J. W. Ferree

The Falls of Niagara and Scenes around them

J. W. Ferree

The Falls of Niagara and Scenes around them

ISBN/EAN: 9783743344945

Manufactured in Europe, USA, Canada, Australia, Japa

Cover: Foto ©Andreas Hilbeck / pixelio.de

Manufactured and distributed by brebook publishing software (www.brebook.com)

J. W. Ferree

The Falls of Niagara and Scenes around them

THE

AND

SCENES AROUND THEM.

BY
J. W. FERREE, A. M.,
PROF. NAT. SCIENCE AND HIGHER MATH. IN STATE NORMAL SCHOOL,
BLOOMSBURG, PA.

PRINTED FOR THE AUTHOR
BY
A. S. BARNES & COMPANY,
111 & 113 WILLIAM STREET, NEW YORK.
1876.

Copyright,
J. W. FERREE,
1876.

TO

My Wife,

WHOSE

SYMPATHY AND AID

IN MY PROFESSIONAL LIFE

HAVE BEEN

My Inspiration,

THIS LITTLE VOLUME

IS

Affectionately Dedicated.

PREFACE.

The author has frequently visited the Falls of Niagara; lingering there, fascinated and irresistibly chained by the grandeur of the mighty cataracts. He has made personal observations from all their various standpoints; treasured an abundance of foot-notes, which have been enriched by varied information from guides at the Falls and resident citizens. He has returned from his rambles, where birds sing and wild flowers grow, laden with rich spoils from all their shady nooks and rocky fortresses.

He therefore claims, in this little volume, some degree of accuracy of statement. He is aware, however, of a discrepancy of opinion, at some points, by diverse pens. Such is the beauty, grandeur, and variety of scenery with which Niagara is crowned, that every attempt to portray it must be diversified. Each is only an essay to paint scenes which baffle description.

To each Niagara conveys its own description. The author writes in the fulness of his subject, and has little apology to make for the style of composition. It cannot have the calm, smoothly-flowing numbers of a plain narrative. The pen, like Niagara itself, breaks down under its own weight. While the author's pen has traced these lines, he has re-communed with the awful, the beautiful, and the grand in Niagara. He is conscious of defects in the following pages, arising from hasty preparation and weighty avocations.

The book, designed for general readers, makes little reference to the geological character of the strata and rocks at Niagara.

The illustrations with which the work is embellished are minutely correct. Some are engravings from photographs, and others are from fine designs, executed on the spot by Washington Friend, Esq., whose beautiful Panorama of American Scenery is well known to the public. The engravings are furnished by the popular house of Messrs. T. Nelson & Sons, New York.

With these brief prefatory remarks, this little volume, with modest pretensions, is sent out in its humble mission, assuring the reader that the following descriptions, however vivid, convey very inadequately an idea of the beauty and grandeur of far-famed Niagara—the Pride of America.

J. W. F.

BLOOMSBURG, PA., *March* 20, 1876.

CONTENTS.

CHAPTER I.
PAGE

Poetry.—The Grandeur of Niagara.—Its Renown.—Visitors.—The Multitudes from Afar.—Its Volume.—Its Beauty and Power.—The Indian name Niagara.—Its Significance.—Poverty of Language and Description.—Its Terror.—The Lakes it Drains.—European and American Scenes.—Its Source and Mouth.—Its Location.—Its Length and Depth.—Difference in Lake Levels...15-22

CHAPTER II.

The Swiftness of Niagara.—Its Breadth.—Grand Island.—Its Area.—Division of the River by Grand Island.—Its Serene Grandeur.—Its Banks.—Islands.—Steamers on the River.—Birds Soaring over the River.—Their Prey.—The River a Great Residence for Wild Fowl.—Flocks of Wild Geese.—Their Long Journeys.—Their Powers of Flight.—"A Wild Goose Chase."..23-26

CHAPTER III.

The Rapids.—Aspect of the River.—Its Tranquillity.—Its Disturbed Repose.—Increased Confusion.—Its Flight.—Contrast. Its Limits.—Its Wrathful Appearance.—Head of the Rapids.—The Roaring of the Falls.—Distance Heard, and Echoes.—Awful Impression.—Goat Island.—Division of the River.—Velocity of the Rapids.—Spray Seen Afar off.—Its Height.—Birds and

Animals in the Rapids.—Trees going over the Falls.—Their Velocity.—Rocks in Rapids.—Depth of Rapids.—Condemned Ship.—Rapids, Why so Called.—Their Descent.—Rocks Submerged.—Tons of Water per Minute.—Homage to Greatness..27–34

CHAPTER IV.

Leaving the Rapids.—Gliding Along the Shore.—Niagara Village. —Distance from Buffalo.—Its Residences, Mansions, Hotels, Scenery. — Coach Drivers. — Interest taken by Coachmen.— Chorus of Voices.—Carpet Bags and Trunks.—Merry Voices. —Hurried Footsteps.—Entranced Passengers...............35–37

CHAPTER V.

The Two Rapids.—Their Volume.—The American Falls.—The Canada, or Horse-Shoe Falls.—Goat Island.—Its Area and Names. — Proprietors.—Daring Visitors.—Their Names and Dates on the Bark of the Trees.—Cast-Iron Bridge.—Its Dimensions.—When and by Whom Built.—Toll Rates.—Mode of Construction.—Bridge near the American Falls.—Lashed by the Rapids.—Spectator Filled with Awe.—He Hurries to the Island.—Roads on the Island.................. 38–41

CHAPTER VI.

Iris Island.—Its Beauty and Verdure.—Its Flowers.—May Day. Its Enchanting Touch.—Flowers in Faultless Combination.— Scenery Beautiful and Varied. — Matchless Harmonies. — Delightful Thoughts and Thrilling Effects.—Trees Crowned with Birds.—Their Plumage and Songs.—Luminous Mist.— Pearly Clouds.—Beauty in Nature.—Beauty in Art.—Beauty Divine.—God its Source.—Beauties yet to be Revealed 42–49

CHAPTER VII.

Visitor Approaches the Falls.—The Mind recoils from its First Vision.—Enchanted with the Grandeur and Sublimity of the Scene.—Configurations of the Spray.—The Falling Sheets.—Pyramids of Egypt.—Rainbows.—Vanishing Forms.—Rivers Pouring Away.—Verge of the Island.—Cautions to Visitors.—Standpoints Beset with Dangers.—Visitors Tempted to Pluck Flowers from the Verge of the Cataracts.—Thrilling Incidents.—Painfully Distressing Occurrences.—Public Expression of Sorrow 50–61

CHAPTER VIII.

Verge of the Island.—Circular Stairway.—When and by Whom Constructed.—Total Height from the River.—Dismal Descent.—Wildness of Scenery.—Impending Rocks.—Fearful Impressions.—Lonely Path.—Rills Overhead.—Ruins.—Little Bird.—Foot of the Falls.—Awful Impressions.—Wrathful Billows.—Gulf-Bottom.—Scenes at each Standpoint.—Rainbows.—Symbols.—The Sun's Alchemy.—Velocity of Falling Sheets.—Visitors Behind the Falls.—Awful Dungeon.—Reflections.—Man's Noblest Structures.—Man Humbled.—His Haughtiness Quenched.. 62–72

CHAPTER IX.

Leaving our Standpoint.—Pass the Biddle Stairway.—Three Falls.—Luna Island.—Lunar Bow.—Origin of Name.—Third or Central Fall.—Foot-Bridge.—" Cave of the Winds."—Origin of Name.—Character of the Rocks.—Table Rock.—Pressure of Water.—Falling Rocks.—Dates.—Deep Gorge cut through Rocks.—Dimensions.—Falls at Queenstown.—Falls Recede and Drain Lake Erie.—Dip of the Rocks.................. 75–78

CHAPTER X.

"Sam Patch."—His Leaps.—Ladder.—Height.—His Leap at Genesee Falls, N. Y.—Reflections.—Change of Position.—Ascend the Tower.—Gliding Along the Verge of Goat Island.—Moss Islands, or Three Sister Islands.—Bridges.—Finest View of the Rapids.—The Hermit's Cascade.—The Stranger's Residence.—Subject to Melancholy.—Cabin.—Flute.—Log projecting over the Falls.—His Homage and Delight.—Bathes and Perishes.—Leave Sister Islands.—Re-cross the Iron Bridge that Spans the Rapids.—Declining Day.—Return to Niagara Village.—Sunset.—Domiciled.—Beauty of Western Sky.—Charming Scenes.—Moral Reflections.................81–85

CHAPTER XI.

Early Dawn.—Toilet and Entertainment.—Village Street.—Beautiful Park.—Stately Oaks.—Avenues.—Promenades.—Pleasure Grounds.—Enchanting Views.—Concert.—Gateways.—Toll.—Point-View.—Banks and Masonry.—Photographing Gallery.—Inclined Railway.—Length and Breadth.—Its Object.—Flight of Steps.—Safe Descent.—Spray Showers.—Third Cavern.—Ferry Boat.—Battling the Billows.—New Suspension Bridge.—Its Location and Description.—Stairway.—Elevator.—Tolls....................................86–95

CHAPTER XII.

The "Maid of the Mist."—Its Terrible and Sublime Mission.—Under the Floods and Spray.—Gorgeous Scenes.—Leave New Suspension Bridge.—Horse-Shoe Falls, Canada Side.—Table Rock.—Gulf Basin.—Scale of Vastness.—Grand Outline.—Behind the Falls.—Companion Behind the Falls.—Spray.—Falling Rocks.—Niagara in Winter.—Ice Crystals.—Configurations.—Brilliant Points.—Forest of Jewels.—Ice Bridge.—

Feelings of Devotion. — Farewell.—Apostrophe to Niagara.—
Legend of the White Canoe.—Museum................96–113

CHAPTER XIII.

Burning Spring.—Light and Heat.—Chippewa.—Battle in 1814.—
Fort Erie.—Battle of Lundy's Lane.--General Winfield Scott's
Victory.—General Scott's Visit.— Flowers.—Navy Island.—
"Patriot's War."—American Sympathy.—President's Proclamation.—The Steamer Caroline.—Seized and Sent over the
Falls.—Her Expiring Lights............................114–117

CHAPTER XIV.

Blondin the Rope Walker. — Rope over the Gulf.—Railway
Trains.—His Marvellous Feats.—Indians.—Their Manufactures.
—Brilliant Colors.—Civilized.--The Great Railway Suspension
Bridge...118–125

CHAPTER XV.

Rapids and Whirlpool.—Sir Charles Lyell.—Devil's Hole.—Bloody
Run. — Brock's Monument. — Queenstown. — Lewiston. — Indians.—Youngstown.................................126–133

CHAPTER XVI.

Henry B. Bascom at Niagara.—Description of Niagara by Charles
Dickens.—Description of Niagara by Professor Tyndall. —
Poetry.....................................134–152

LIST OF ILLUSTRATIONS.

	PAGE
1. *Frontispiece*—Great Railway Suspension Bridge	1
2. American Falls	34
3. Cast-Iron Bridge and Rapids above the Falls	43
4. Horse-Shoe Falls from Goat Island	51
5. Horse-Shoe Falls from the Floor of the River	63
6. Whirlwind Bridge, Rock of Ages, and Cave of the Winds	74
7. Three Sisters and Goat Island from Canada Side	80
8. Niagara Falls from Point Prospect—American Side	87
9. New Suspension Bridge—Niagara	97
10. Niagara in Winter from Canada Side	106
11. The Whirlpool Rapids—Niagara	127
12. Brock's Monument and Niagara River looking towards Lake Ontario	131

CHAPTER I.

Poetry—The Grandeur of Niagara—Its Renown—Visitors—The Multitudes from Afar—Its Volume—Its Beauty and Power—The Indian name Niagara—Its Significance—Poverty of Language and Description—Its Terror—The Lakes it Drains—European and American Scenes—Its Source and Mouth—Its Location—Its Length and Breadth—Difference in Lake Levels.

NIAGARA.

FLOW on forever, in thy glorious robe
Of terror and of beauty. Yea, flow on,
Unfathomed and resistless. God hath set
His rainbow on thy forehead, and the cloud
Mantled around thy feet. And He doth give
Thy voice of thunder power to speak of Him
Eternally—bidding the lip of man
Keep silence, and upon thine altar pour
Incense of awe-struck praise.
     Earth fears to lift
The insect trump that tells her trifling joys
Or fleeting triumphs, 'mid the peal sublime

Of thy tremendous hymn. Proud Ocean shrinks
Back from thy brotherhood, and all his waves
Retire abashed. For he hath need to sleep,
Sometimes, like a spent laborer, calling home
His boisterous billows, from their vexing play,
To a long, dreary calm : but thy strong tide
Faints not, nor e'er with failing heart forgets
Its everlasting lesson, night nor day.
The morning stars, that hailed Creation's birth,
Heard thy hoarse anthem mixing with their song
Jehovah's name ; and the dissolving fires,
That wait the mandate of the day of doom
To wreck the Earth, shall find it deep inscribed
Upon thy rocky scroll.
  * * * * *
      Lo ! yon birds,
How bold ! they venture near, dipping their wing
In all thy mist and foam. Perchance 'tis meet
For them to touch thy garment's hem, or stir
Thy diamond wreath, who sport upon the cloud
Unblamed, or warble at the gate of heaven
Without reproof. But as for us, it seems
Scarce lawful with our erring lips to talk
Familiarly of thee. Methinks, to trace
Thine awful features with our pencil's point
Were but to press on Sinai.
       Thou dost speak

Alone of God, who poured thee as a drop
From His right hand—bidding the soul that looks
Upon thy fearful majesty be still,
Be humbly wrapped in its own nothingness,
And lose itself in Him.
                                Mrs. Sigourney.

The Falls of Niagara are the monarchs of cataracts. Their volume, grandeur, and sublimity, tower far above all other cataracts. They are pre-eminent and sovereign. They are world-renowned, and are linked with stupendous transactions. They attract the man of science, as well as the wonder-loving tourist and the enthusiastic admirer of sublime scenery. They allure more visitors than any other natural curiosity on the globe.

Tidings of Niagara, from afar, bring hither the legions. From every clime—east, west, north, and south—the highways are thronged with travelers to their dominions, to pay unresisting homage to their majesty and supremacy. Eager multitudes, on stretch of expectation, throng the dusty highways, and hurry hither, in marching columns, where fame has noised abroad, world-wide, the grandeur of Niagara. They come from the continents; the islands of the ocean; the mountains, valleys, and plains, to gaze in speechless wonder and admiration upon the world's greatest, renowned spectacle. Untold myriads have resorted hither, and bowed in adoring wonder before such grand displays of inimitable beauty and matchless power.

From the hot walls and hotter streets of the cities, summer tourists hurry to join the tide of travel, seeking the natural wonders, cool retreats, and delights of Niagara.

Niagara transcends all other rivers that roll along the horizon of history. All feast on its grandeur and beauty, which no pen can sketch, and description only dwarfs. The imagination kindles at the name, and we fancy at once that we are borne away into their enchanted regions. We see them, or fancy we see them, and are absorbed in coveted visions of their grandeur. Magically, whether in fact or fancy, we are charmed and amazed.

The Indian term "Niagara" is expressive. Its significance is well disclosed in the phrase, "Thunder of Waters." Indian words are imprints of vocal sounds. The Indian mind is exceedingly rich and significant in coining expressive words to type natural objects. Words are thought-symbols. If audible, they are voice-sounds.

Words are thoughts crystallized. Hence, language is a mirror of objects. It is historic, filtering down through the ages, carrying forward the knowledge of all that man has done. How expressive is the term Niagara—"Thunder of Waters"! The word will entomb the thought, not only while the Falls themselves shall endure, but long after they shall cease to be.

Niagara remains alone. The usual exhibitions of natural phenomena, heightened by some scale of comparative sublimity, delight us. But new scenes kindle the imagination and arouse curiosity. Unusual displays, combining the beautiful and the terrible, startle and appal us. The boldest cowers; the bravest shrinks. Such is Niagara. It drains the waters of four great North American lakes—Lake Superior, Lake Michigan, Lake Huron, and Lake Erie—containing an area of one hundred thousand square miles, and an average depth of one thousand feet, and hurls their dreadful torrents over precipices one hundred and seventy feet into fathomless depths below. The haughty mountain billows then gush up without measure from the boiling deep; roll and foam in their liquid beds; lash the shores; proudly exulting in the magnificence of their own display. Desolating blasts preside over the terrific scene, and sweep their gales with destructive fury.

Europe justly boasts of her cragged mountains; her noble, meandering rivers; her magnificent lakes; her endless succession of hills, clothed with forests, and gentle slopes covered with olives and vines; her valleys, remarkable for wild, romantic beauty; her rich mineral treasures, and the fertility of her soil. She yields to none in general grandeur and sublime scenery.

Americans who have visited that enchanting continent, have fully realized the beauty of the picture. The pen of the poet and the pencil of the artist have not adorned it with tints denied it by the hand of nature. Those who have lingered most around its far-spread wonders and beauties, have not been surprised at enthusiasm thus sanctioned by reality.

Separated, however, from the Old World by an intervening ocean, the American feels that he has lakes rolling their waves in grandeur over a vaster expanse; greater rivers, flowing through more extensive tracts; mountains more massive, towering, and venerable with snow; landscapes enriched by wilder prospects, and embellished with more varied scenery; caverns hung with stalactites and jewels; grottoes unsounded by human plummet, and sparkling with transparent crystals; crevices richer with veins of silver and gold; recesses filled with gems, amethysts, rubies, and diamonds; skies enkindled by as bright sunshine; clouds painted by as beautiful rainbows; and mightier cataracts thundering down into deeper chasms.

Niagara is unlike other rivers in its source. It has not its origin in deep well-springs or numerous rivulets issuing from mountain slopes, then swelled by larger streams in its progress toward the sea. Its source is in the eastern extremity of Lake Erie, and its mouth in Lake Ontario. It is rather a mighty, natural aqueduct, or channel, conveying the waters of the upper lakes to Lake Ontario.

The Niagara river is thirty-four miles long, and flows in a northerly direction. It separates, in part, western New York and Canada. It is of great depth, and constantly swelled to a calm fulness by the vast influx of waters from the West. Its source is in the vicinity of the great commercial city of Buffalo, western New York; from which to the Falls it is twenty-two miles. The difference, in level, between its source and mouth, or between the surfaces of the two lakes (Erie and Ontario) is three hundred and thirty-five feet. The line of railroad travel is principally along both margins of the river, passing through fertile plains, abounding with productive farms, fine villages, and beautiful residences.

Fine views of the river are seen from the railroad track, as the train of passenger cars sweeps on from the city of Buffalo, or Fort Erie (Canada side), to the Falls. The eye gazes upon its grand and beautiful features, as it rolls smoothly on, and stretches far away in its lines of magnificent distances.

CHAPTER II.

The Swiftness of Niagara—Its Breadth—Grand Island—Its Area—Division of Niagara by Grand Island—Its Serene Grandeur—Its Banks—Islands—Steamers on the River—Birds Soaring over the River—Their Prey—Grand Residence for Wild Fowl—Wild Geese—Their Long Journeys—Their Powers of Flight—"A Wild Goose Chase."

THE current of the river is swift the first two miles from Lake Erie. It then flows more gently, widens, and divides into two arms that embrace Grand Island. This beautiful island is twelve miles long, from two to seven miles wide, and extends within three miles of the Falls. As these two branches again unite, below the island, the river expands from two to three miles in breadth. It now moves on silently, in majesty and pride, in apparently conscious grandeur and overwhelming power.

The river is studded with a very large number of low islands, seeming to rest on its bosom, exquisitely beautiful, rich in soil, and luxuriant in vegetation. Steamers ply between Buffalo city and the village of Chippewa (Canada side), within two miles and a half of the Falls. They venture no further down the river.

In the upper part of the river the banks vary from twenty to thirty feet in height, and the general current is moderate. There is no flood-ground, or overflow of the river. It is unvarying in its fulness—never increasing, and never diminishing, except when the waters of the lake are forced into it under the action of heavy gales of winds from the west. From this cause, in the spring of 1847, it rose six feet perpendicularly in the Rapids.

With the otherwise unchanging depth of twenty-five feet, the crystal river, imaging objects overhanging the banks, glides peacefully along in serene grandeur; winding through landscapes in graceful curves, presenting as smooth a surface as reflects from the glassy bosom of the ocean deep. The sun, moon, stars, clouds, and sky, are beautifully mirrored in its polished surface.

Birds, gifted with unwearied powers of flight, are incessantly soaring over the river, in quest of fish. When they perceive their prey, they dart down with surprising velocity, and generally bear up a struggling fish in their talons.

Like a beautifully expanded lake, the river furnishes grand residences for various kinds of aquatic wild fowl. Great flocks of wild geese, on their long spring journeys, of extraordinary speed, from south to north, and on their return in autumn, often descend to the river, and for a time float and bathe in their downy majesty on the bosom of its waters. Afar off, and at immense heights, sweeping through the ocean of air, the keen vision of these migratory birds catches the glassy expanse of the distant, smoothly-rolling river. They are rapid and powerful fliers. Such are their enduring powers of flight, through the boundless sky, that, at almost invisible heights, for days, unwearied, their wings fan the illimitable air. Sometimes their height is so great that their individual forms are lost, and the figure only of the mighty aerial caravan is seen. They are often heard, when they are so high as to be invisible. They fly in the form of the letter V, in lines moving in the direction of the point of the letter. When arranged, each one keeps its place in the ranks. If the male bird at the head becomes fatigued, it retires to the rear, and the second one takes the lead. When they sleep, one is always on the watch, to give the alarm at the approach of danger. From their vigilance in this respect, they are difficult to catch. Hence the saying, "a wild-goose chase," indicating a hopeless pursuit.

CHAPTER III.

The Rapids—Aspect of the River—Its Tranquillity—Its Disturbed Repose—Increased Confusion—Its Flight—The Contrast—Its Limits—Its Wrathful Appearance—Head of the Rapids—Roaring of the Falls—Distance Heard, and Echoes—Awful Impression—Goat Island—Division of the River—Velocity of the Rapids—Spray Seen Afar off—Its Height—Birds and Animals in the Rapids—Trees Going over the Falls—Their Velocity—Rocks in the Rapids—Depth of Rapids—Condemned Ship—Rapids, Why so Called—Their Descent—Rocks Submerged—Tons of Water per Minute—Homage to Greatness.

AS far as the range of vision sweeps, the river majestically rolls on its crystal waters, like an immense mirror of burnished silver. Adieu, Beautiful River! Thou art the grandest that has rolled down through the ages.

We are approaching the Rapids. The river is beginning to change its aspect. It is contracting its limits to three-quarters of a mile in breadth. Its increasingly disturbed tranquillity foreshadows coming events—heralds dangers near. It is assuming, more and more, an irritable, wrathful aspect, which the sea must exhibit when suddenly swept by the burst of a tempest.

Having been long treasured, or quietly imbosomed in the great lakes; and having, apparently, gathered strength from extended repose, and tranquilly drawn from these capacious reservoirs; it seems, at first, to manifest an indisposition to increased activity.

Like the writhings of an angry serpent, suddenly aroused by the destroyer, its repose is disquieted. It recoils from its approaching destiny. It reels, boils, and is stirred to its depths. Having so long passively yielded to presiding powers, it now reasserts its supremacy; becomes fretful; hurls off restraints; covets confusion and destruction; and takes its flight from plains, landscapes, flowers, cultivated fields, rich pastures, flocks, and the busy abodes of men.

What a contrast! A little while ago, it was unruffled, and smooth as polished marble; now, it is turbulent, noisy, and arrayed in a phase of threatening awfulness.

We now stand at the head of the Rapids, on the American side (improperly called), and are within one-half mile of the Falls. Their booming roar already quakes the ground beneath our feet. They are sometimes heard at Toronto (capital of Canada West), a distance of fifty miles. Their far-off echoes come back like the roll of distant thunder.

We gaze upon the terrific scene around us, and are dumb. In silence, we only wonder and adore.

Like a dreadful, heaving sea, the deep river swells, and bears on its turbulent billows into the profound gulfs below. Their wildness and magnitude make an impression of imposing grandeur.

Here, at the head of the Rapids, and also at the head of Iris, or Goat Island (which extends to the cataracts), the river sets off, or divides, into two branches (themselves large rivers) embracing and sweeping round Goat Island, and uniting again below the Falls, at the foot of Goat Island. One of these branches washes the American shore, and the other branch the Canada shore.

These branch-rivers form the half-mile Rapids. They start off like racers in their sublime course, swiftly descending their inclined beds with a velocity of sixty feet a second, or forty miles an hour (less by reason of resistances from flexures and friction).

Afar off is seen, in the direction of the Falls an exhaustless profusion of great white clouds, rising up majestically, as if they came from the depths of the earth. They ascend like massive columns of thick smoke from the terrible conflagration of a city. The spray is sometimes seen at a distance of one hundred miles. It is then more than a mile above the Falls.

Flocks of aquatic birds, swimming in the river above the Falls, sometimes enter the Rapids, and are carried down with such incredible swiftness that it is impossible for them to rise from the current. When approaching the Falls, they are sometimes seen to struggle to take wing and leave the water. But they cannot. Hence, they are hurled over the Falls and perish.

Fish, deer, bears, cattle, and other animals, aiming to cross the river above, are sometimes drawn into the Rapids, and are borne down the angry floods, and are ingulfed in the terrible abyss below. It is said the larger animals found below are crushed to pieces. Resident citizens at the Falls say there has been an instance or two in which an animal has gone over the Falls, and yet survived.

Trees, which for ages have stood on the banks of the river, sometimes become disengaged from the soil, by the incessant washings of their roots, and bolt down the torrents over the Falls with

Scenes Around Them.

such amazing velocity that they are never seen afterwards.

Large rocks, also, loosened or uptorn from their beds, are borne along the resistless tide with a heavy roar; strike other buried rocks; loom up for a moment above the flood, like some huge monster, and then are violently hurled into the measureless chasm.

One moment some object is seen climbing and towering upon the crest of a billow, then sinking in the gulf below and extinguished forever.

Some estimate of the depth of the Rapids may be obtained from an incident that occurred many years ago. The ship Michigan, with a hull of twenty feet, was condemned, in 1827, as unseaworthy, and was sent over the Falls. It filled in the Rapids on the Canada side, and was completely submerged. It passed down the Rapids, and over the precipice, without touching bottom.

The Rapids are so called because the river here has a descent of sixty feet in the half mile. The current, quickened in its velocity, becomes wild with action, and, storming in madness, is hurled into rapids, whirlpools, and eddies.

Myriads of huge rocks, in apparently conscious strength, interspersed and slumbering in the beds of these Rapids, break, in some degree, the waters in their downward flight, varying the direction of their channels, and forcing them into abrupt sinuosities.

These obstructions cause the high, swelling surfs to break in confusion, rebound, and pile themselves around the ponderous rocks, whose flinty summits, in turn, sever the drenching waves, and fling them shapelessly in every direction. The billows foam, toss, and tumble; breaking over the rocks in such endless forms, and in such perpetual variety, as never to weary the eye.

Thus, onward rushes Niagara, in savage grandeur, like a deep, heaving sea, bounding and rebounding with terrible impetuosity down its rocky bed, while sea-like sheets of emerald dash and tower aloft in fantastic shapes, then descend in scattered showers of liquid pearls. Sporting waves, white-crested in turmoils of foam, fill the air with silvery spray, terribly disclosing their majesty and power. The scene, grand and dreadful, thrills the beholder with awe, as he gazes, spell-bound, on this frightful power, sweeping onward its vast floods of twelve millions of tons a minute into the abysmal gulfs below. He surveys with dumb admiration its half-comprehended grandeur, and sinks into nothingness, yielding the deep homage that mind pays to greatness.

AMERICAN FALLS.

CHAPTER IV.

Leaving the Rapids—Gliding Along the Shore—Niagara Village—Distance from Buffalo—Its Residences, Mansions, Hotels, Scenery—Coach Drivers—Interest Taken in Travellers—Chorus of Voices—Carpet Bags and Trunks—Merry Voices—Hurried Footsteps—Entranced Passengers.

WE now leave our present standpoint, at the head of the Rapids, and file our way down along the eastern shore of the Rapids (American side) to the village, called Niagara Falls. It is in the immediate vicinity of the cataracts, and somewhat imbosomed among the trees. The village is twenty-two miles by rail from the city of Buffalo, the eastern point of Lake Erie. It contains many elegant private residences; fine, tasteful mansions; and a number of first-class hotels.

The general appearance of the country around the village is rugged, romantic, and grand.

Niagara being a place of great fashionable resort, its scenery is one of constant bustle and animation. Long before the arrival of the trains, the usual array of omnibuses, cabs, carriages, and all other wheeled conveyances—in short, every means of transit—are most plentifully on hand at the depot, anxiously awaiting the arrival of the trains.

What an animated spectacle! What busy scenes! What a throng of elegant equipages! What competitions for the luxury of passengers in beautifully curtained and crimson-cushioned carriages, to transfer visitors to the elegant hotels.

Before the car-wheels cease their revolutions, or the passenger alights from the train, a shout of voices goes up from the coach-drivers: "Gentlemen, who's for the Cataract Hotel?" And another: "Carriage, gentlemen, for the Spencer House." "Free carriage, gentlemen," cries another, "to the International Hotel; it is the best house." "Who is for the various points of interest about the Falls, gentlemen?" cries another. Now sets in a general chorus of voices, in mingled harmonies: "Only one dollar, gentlemen and ladies, for a carriage to the great Suspension Bridge." "Who is for the Whirlpool, gentlemen?" "The Burning Spring?" "The battle of Lundy's Lane?" "The Bloody Run?" "Queenstown Heights?" "Brock's Monument?" "The Rapids?" "The Devil's Hole?" &c., &c.

A watchful eye of the passenger on his baggage is needful, else his trunk and carpet-bag, through the excessive kindness of carriages, will be on their way to the hotels, ahead of the rightful owner. In all these hotels visitors may anticipate hearty welcomes and every comfort by their gentlemanly and cultivated proprietors.

Guides, eloquently gifted, furnish visitors graphic descriptions of all the various standpoints about the Falls.

Everywhere in the busy streets is heard the hum of merry voices and the tread of hurried footsteps. Glittering carriages, filled with entranced passengers, hastily diverge in every direction, to visit the various surrounding scenes of interest.

CHAPTER V.

The Two Rapids—Their Volume—The American Falls—The Horse-Shoe Falls (Canada side)—Goat Island—Its Area and Names—Proprietors—Daring Visitors—Their Names and Dates on the Bark of Trees—Cast-Iron Bridge—Its Dimensions—When and by Whom Built—Toll Rates—Mode of Construction—Bridge near the American Falls—Lashed by the Rapids—Spectator Filled with Awe—He Hurries to the Island—Roads on the Island.

THE two Rapids are not equal in area and volume. The Rapids on the Canada side are much the larger. The American Falls are reckoned about one thousand feet in breadth, and one hundred and seventy feet in height. The Falls on the Canada side are about two thousand feet in breadth, and one hundred and sixty feet in height. The Falls on the Canada side are curved in the form of a horse-shoe; hence they are called the Horse-Shoe Falls. The open part of the shoe points down the river. The total breadth of the two Falls, including the verge of Goat Island (that intervenes between them) is about five thousand feet.

Scenes Around Them.

Goat Island extends to the cataracts and divides them. Its verge is in a line with the Falls. The island is about one-half mile in length and one-quarter of a mile in breadth, and contains about seventy acres. In 1770 a man by the name of Stedman pastured some goats on it; hence its name. It is also called Iris, or Rainbow Island, from the rainbows that play in the spray of the Falls.

The island has long been in the possession of the Porter family. Judge Porter lays the world under obligation for the great interest he has taken in this island, in affording the many facilities for enjoyment in visiting the Island and the Falls.

At a very early day, long before the bridges to the island were constructed, some daring strangers had, in some way, reached the island, and chronicled the various dates of their visits by the usual practice of cutting figures on the bark of the trees. They must have crossed the Rapids from the American side to the head of the island in boats—which were most dangerous experiments.

We now wend our way to the lower part of the village, to the bridge that spans the American Rapids. There is no bridge spanning the Canada

Rapids. One extremity of the bridge rests on the American shore, and the other extremity on Goat Island. It is constructed of iron, and is three hundred and sixty feet long. It has four arches of ninety feet span each. It is twenty-seven feet broad. It has a double carriage-way, sixteen and one-half feet wide; and two foot-paths, five and one-half feet wide. It was built in 1856, by the Messrs. Porter, proprietors of the island. Judge Porter had constructed a bridge in 1817, further up the Rapids, but it was carried away by an ice-flood. Visitors cross and recross this bridge, as many times a day as they wish, for fifty cents; or, by paying one dollar, they may have the complete use of it for the season.

The foundation of the bridge was laid by constructing a massive pier very near the shore, and then projecting long, heavy timbers on this pier, extending far out over the waters. The heavy beams were firmly secured on shore by piling on them heavy stones and rocks. A number of these beams, side by side, formed a scaffold. The ends over the water were made steady by dropping down under them stilts, securely thrust in the bed of the river. Along this platform heavy stones and rocks were carried and dropped down into the Rapids, thus forming a base, or second pier, and so on. In like manner they platformed, or bridged, the entire Rapids from the shore to the island. The Iron Bridge, completely finished by spans, followed immediately in the wake of the platforms. It is within a stone's throw of the yawning gulf.

Beneath this bridge coiled rivers lash and foam dreadfully terrible. They come down like mountain torrents, having the speed of an arrow. It seems to waver from the violent surges beating against it. The spectator is filled with horror, as the eye looks down upon the angry, rushing flood, threatening to sweep the bridge from its frail foundations and hurl it over the dreadful precipice. The trembling visitor hastens onward to plant his foot upon the shore of Iris Island. Here is a picturesque cottage, in which visitors record their names.

From the end of the bridge three roads diverge. The first immediately crosses the island. The second, to the left, reaches to the head of the island. The third, to the right, leads to the Falls. A road also sweeps entirely around the island.

The visitor now stands upon Iris Island, with the magnificent river above him, the Rapids on each side of him, and the Falls before him.

CHAPTER VI.

Iris Island—Its Beauty and Verdure—Its Flowers—May Day—Its Enchanting Touch—Flowers—Scenery—Matchless Harmonies—Delightful Thoughts—Thrilling Effects—Trees Crowned with Birds—Their Plumage and Songs—Luminous Mist—Pearly Clouds—Beauty in Nature—Beauty in Art—Beauty Divine—God its Source—Beauties to be Revealed.

IRIS Island is of sylvan loveliness. It is highly picturesque, clad in robes of luxuriant verdure. It is thickly set with stately, graceful trees of richest foliage. On some the foliage gleams with flakes of emerald; while on others, many-hued, it glitters brilliantly.

Flowers, whose delicious perfumes are wafted afar, embellish the island. Our present visit was on a beautiful day in the lovely month of May, and the whole island was in a floral blaze, richly entitled to and challenging our highest admiration.

At the bidding of May, the foliage and flowers blended their richly-colored tints in such faultless

CAST IRON BRIDGE AND RAPIDS ABOVE THE FALLS.

Scenes Around Them. 45

combinations that the painter's highest art would despair to imitate. Her enchanted touch unveiled the blush of flowers in their richest crimson, purple, and gold.

The whole scenery was an emerald expanse, set and embellished with floral stars in their full glory. When agitated by the breeze, under the full splendors of the sun, their petals gleamed with purple, azure, gold, and crimson, presenting the appearance of beautifully colored flame. Glorious realm! in which are beautifully enshrined the glory and grandeur of the Creator. Here, surrounded by these wild and awful scenes, Nature lavishes her paradise of loveliness, revealing herself in fascinating expressions of the wonderful and the beautiful.

Even on the very verge of the precipice, majestic trees, in pomp and splendor, loom up, and, standing on these terrible thresholds, scorn the feet that dare venture upon their untrodden solitudes. Nature blends her works in matchless harmonies. All the scenes around thrill and exhilarate. Tides of emotions rush through the soul, and deepen the sensibilities. Enchantment kindles delightful thoughts, which enrich beauty and enrapture the heart.

Each tree seemed to be crowned and its boughs

bending with the weight of numerous birds of gorgeous plumage and exquisite song. Some, on elastic wing, were flitting to and fro from the summits of the trees. Some were fluttering on tremulous wing, then gently descending upon the grassy lawn. Others were gayly hopping on the ground. Others, still, were perching on slender, fragile twigs overhanging the frightful torrent.

Beautiful birds! What brilliant colors! What reflections of beauty! How richly adorned with plumage that vies the rainbow tints. Delightful banquet of birds! Their entertainment wins the admiration of every eye. How full of life and activity! How elegant their forms! How graceful in all their movements! What sweet songs and rich utterances warble from their throats! Each one, full of song, seems to exult with delight, as if overcome with joy and ecstacy in greeting the numerous strangers, welcoming the arrival of visitors, and hymning sweet anthems of praise to their Creator.

Myriads, too, of humming, gaudy-winged insects mingle with the foliage and the flowers.

Afar off are seen luminous mist and pearly clouds, peering up through the trees and foliage, glowing with brilliant tints and gleaming with indescribable beauty. Now the vapor rises in rich confusion on the tremulous air, dissolves, and quickly vanishes. Then again, in quick succession other forms, as richly adorned, spring up in their delicate fabrics, but, evanescent as before, are rapidly transformed, and invisibly lost in thin air. Thus new creations, in ever-varying forms, thrill the spectator with pleasure and delight.

The scenery all around is unmatched for wild, romantic beauty and sublime splendor, and throws over the spectator its spell of inspiration. On every side, resistless fascinations surround him.

The hills stretch far away in enchanting prospects. The distant landscapes beguile him. The trees shine in their emerald robes, intermingling in richest varieties with orange and red. The green lawn glistens with roseate pearls, and exhales a delightful fragrance from aromatic herbs. The grove is enchanting with the melody of birds, beautifully replumed in their feathery robes. The surging rapids, in roaring floods, are sweeping around him. The thunders of the Cataracts are echoed in answering thunders from the hills and skies. The gulfs are before him.

The sun pours down his unusually bright beams, as if to renew his splendor, and more fully illumine and adorn the surrounding scenery. Rainbows, enshrined in the mist, painting the spray, rise up as if to embellish the wardrobe of the skies.

The visitor is captivated by such new, unusual displays of charming combinations in their richest varieties. His joyous feelings run at high tide. He is enshrined in beauty and wonder. The treasures of beauty, in lavished abundance, enravish the mind with visions of indescribable loveliness.

Nature is the parent of beauty. She fashions her works—moulds and embellishes her forms—upon exquisite models.

The mind delights in beauty. It loves rapid transitions from one extreme to another: from shadows to lights; from the ridiculous to the sublime; from deformity to elegance; and from wild magnificence to a mild radiance. It recoils at ugly forms and jarring discordances.

Every beautiful object reveals the Infinite. Material beauty is the reflection of spiritual beauty. Beauty blends the finite with the infinite. The visible and the invisible combine. Beauty in thought is unfolded and expressed in beauty in Art. Hence, in human designs, the highest realms of art evolve the highest manifestations of beauty.

God is the only source of material and spiritual beauty. Beauty is a thing divine.

This godlike gift is innate, and ministers to purposes higher than utility. It touches our finest sensibilities, and refines our highest enjoyments. The soul thirsts for beauty. When it fills the eye and enraptures the ear, it only awakens a thirst for the still higher beautiful. Her domain covets our highest tastes. The realms of cultivated taste will forever widen, leading the soul upward. Now, the outward but awakens it.

The treasures of beauty are not half explored. Other worlds are yet to reveal to us their wondrous beauties, their ravishing sights, and their entrancing harmonies.

What scenes of unveiled beauty shall be revealed to the glorified! What sublime and enchanting disclosures " that eye hath not seen, nor ear heard," shall greet and entrance the spirit in the gateway of the skies. Beauty shall forever heighten, as we are "changed from glory to glory," in beatific visions, and our ears are entranced with richest music from the seraph's harp-strings.

CHAPTER VII.

Visitor Approaches the Falls—The Mind Recoils from its First Vision—Enchanted with the Grandeur of the Scene—Configurations of the Spray—The Falling Sheets—Pyramids of Egypt—Rainbows—Vanishing Forms—Rivers Pouring Away—Verge of the Island—Cautions to Visitors—Standpoints Beset with Dangers—Flowers on the Verge of the Cataracts—Thrilling Incidents—Painfully Distressing Events—Public Expression of Sorrow.

BUT the tourist has not yet gazed upon the world's greatest and grandest spectacle—the Falls of Niagara.

Completing his rambles among the delightful groves of the island, in transport, mingled with anxiety and pleasing fear, he now advances with hurried yet cautious step to realize his first gaze of the Falls of Niagara. With reverential awe, he advances amid terror, beauty, and grandeur. Throbs of trembling expectation and tidal emotions fill the soul.

When the grand drama first opens to his vision,

HORSE-SHOE FALL FROM GOAT ISLAND

he is filled with commingled emotions of grandeur and sublimity, of surprise and astonishment. They far surpass the highest ideal he had entertained of them. Here mingle enchantingly the terrific, the powerful, and the beautiful.

The mind recoils and shrinks from the extraordinary display of wondrous power, so magnificently spread out before it. The bewildered emotions first subside, before the spectator fully realizes the grandeur of the scene before him. Imagination fails to paint such overwhelming powers, suddenly disclosed to the eye, as it looks down into the measureless gulf.

From both Falls, now in full view, we see misty exhalations, in beautiful colonnades of snowy whiteness, tinged with roseate hues, starting up and purpling the sky with iris tints.

The splendor of the sun illumines the deep obscurity that hangs over the scene; changing its gloom into a brilliant diorama, glittering with designs of Divine beauty and Almighty power.

Enchanted and tireless, he gazes upon the gorgeous vapors and seething ocean, blanched to purest whiteness in its swift descent. On the snowy mass of curling mists effulgent rainbows undulate in broken forms and bright arches, too varied for description.

What an abounding prodigality of varied splendor and beauty! The Pyramids of Egypt, in beauty and grandeur, dwarf into insignificance before these Divine creations. What endless scrolls and various forms of glowing images they assume!

Stupendous misty mountain-clouds, rose-touched, loom up, like mighty cathedrals, crowned with domes and steeples. Now we see magnificent palaces—temples of royalty, adorned with lofty towers and spires. Now we perceive various architectural designs—columns of pearl robed in brighter glories than adorn Tyrian princes. Then fling open beautiful gate-ways, and give us inner views of painted palaces, sparkling with misty crystals, snow-white, pearly, and iridescent.

Sometimes the commingling mists assume human resemblances—living forms in panoplies of celestial fabrics—clad in gorgeous robes the glorified wear.

The fanciful forms are often so familiar, and so replete with enduring beauty, that they seem realities. These vanishing, others start up in curiously wrought, grotesque figures, in ever-varying forms.

Thus, like a series of grand, beautifully dissolving views, their diversity and novelty amuse, and awaken the highest pleasure and admiration.

Far below, the smoking floods, like Parian marble, are blanched to whiteness, long before they reach the bottom of the chasm.

The mighty rivers are seen pouring over the perpendicular precipices in vast, magnificent curves, down into the deep gulf-basins, where they are treasured but a moment, then bound off in billows, as if in the joys of recovered freedom.

Thus they are perpetually pouring themselves away, and yet ever renewing, in endless complexities of forms, motions, and beauties.

We now stand upon the verge of the island, between the two Falls, which are seen tumbling on the right and left. Between the two Falls a narrow path skirts the verge of the island, one hundred and eighty-five feet perpendicular above the floor of the river. Flowers are strewed along the very brink of this path, looking down into the deep gulf. Caution is everywhere needful about the Falls, as the various standpoints are beset with frightful precipices and yawning chasms. Every point forewarns the spectator to take the utmost precaution, lest the very attractions decoy the visitor to points in which he is environed in danger too late to escape.

The Falls of Niagara;

Spectators, despite the danger, are sometimes tempted, at the risk of life, to plant the poised foot on the very edge of the rugged, crumbling cliffs, to pluck flowers which nature has placed there only for the pleasure of the zephyrs.

Thrilling incidents are narrated of some who have braved the danger, imperiled their lives, and, for a flower, have gone irrevocably over the precipice into the gulf below.

A melancholy incident of this occurred in 1844, in the case of Miss Rugg. Leaving, for a moment, the arm of her gentleman companion, she ventured to pluck some flowers growing on the edge of Table Rock, on the verge of the Falls, Canada side. The ground immediately gave way beneath her feet; she gave one piercing shriek, and her companion, grasping after her, caught her shawl only, which gave way, and she was precipitated down a perpendicular height of one hundred and twenty feet upon a bed of rocks. The visitors rushed down the spiral stairway to her rescue, and, strange to say, found her yet alive. She faintly whispered, "Pick me up," and expired.

In 1849 there was another scene of dreadful tragedy. A young, joyous company were skirting the edge of the Rapids, just above the Falls, when a young man playfully caught a young lady, saying, under a pretence, that he was going to throw her into the stream. By a sudden impulse she bounded away from him, and fell into the current. In a moment he plunged in after her. Locked in each other's arms, Charles Addington and Annette Deforest were hurled over the dreadful precipice.

The horrified group witnessed the agony of their countenances, as they turned imploringly for help. Their mangled remains were afterwards found in the "Cave of the Winds," American side. The mother of Annette, who had joined the gay company, was near by, and beheld the scene. But she did not long survive the shock. Clad in sorrow, with a broken heart, she soon departed to join her loved one in the better land.

Another case is that of a little child of a poor woman. The mother was washing near the Rapids, and her little child was playing in a tub near by. Unperceived by the mother, it floated out, and was soon beyond her reach. It had entered the Rapids. The little voyager passed over the cataract, while the screams of the mother were drowned by its incessant roar.

The author could furnish a score of similar incidents, but refrains from such distressing references, after giving but one more; for it is too painful to dwell upon these sad occurrences.

In 1853, Joseph Avery and his companion were out one night in a boat in the river, above the Falls. By some means they entered the Rapids, and were swiftly borne toward the cataract (American side). The boat upset in these fearfully surging billows, and his companion was hurled over the Falls, and was seen no more.

Avery, in his descent, accidentally struck a log which had lodged against a rock, and to which he clung through the night. The morning dawned, and a cry of alarm resounded through the village, "A man in the Rapids!"

For a whole day the struggle was continued, with alternate hopes and fears, by thousands of persons, to rescue the pitiable man from the jaws of destruction.

Not only were the sympathies of the citizens of the village and vicinity profoundly awakened in his behalf, but even distant cities and States were aroused with deepest interest, as the winged messages from Niagara conveyed the sad tidings along the wires. Throughout the length and breadth of the land the public heart throbbed with emotions of gratitude towards those whose merciful offices of affection were exercised for his relief. The feelings of the nation spontaneously rose and fell with the despatches bearing intelligence of their alternate successes and defeats. Thousands crowded the telegraphic offices, eager to catch the softest whispers from the telegrams borne along the wires during the vanishing hours of the day.

Boats were lowered towards him, with strong ropes, but were ingulfed before they reached him. Repeated efforts in this way proved only absolutely fruitless. Nothing could stem the mighty torrent.

Hopes were again kindled as the city of Buffalo sent down a life-boat by a swift engine. It was floated down, secured by stout ropes, held by a host of strong, willing men, and was just within his reach, when the angry, heartless billows, scorning his rescue, quickly dashed it off on the neighboring billows and submerged it.

Again all hopes were well nigh extinguished. To encourage the despairing man, the large letters, "We will save you," were painted on a board and exposed to his view.

What earthly situation, by any possibility, could be more cheerless and appalling than this? Dwelling amidst Niagara's terrible thunders, with angry floods all around him, and a yawning gulf almost beneath him!

All, however, eagerly cherished the hope, or desired to cherish it, that "while there is life there is hope." Unwearied in their efforts, another boat was launched, and reached him in safety. Hope now gleamed in every face, as they joyfully exclaimed, "He is saved! He is saved!"

But again, most sadly, it was found that the rope had so caught between the log and rock that all efforts to disengage it proved utterly unavailing. For hours the pitiable man toiled to loosen it. But the strain upon the rope, by the men above, pulling it, broke it.

Again, joyous hopes were crushed. Yet, still untiring in devising means for his rescue, a raft of timbers was next constructed, with a large empty cask at each corner, firmly secured, and ropes attached to the raft, so that he could tie himself safely to it. It was lowered, and reached him just right. He got on it, and every heart again revived and became light. The ropes were carefully drawn in, and the raft was swinging grandly over the billows in promising safety to the shore. But now the large rope holding the raft caught in a ledge of rocks, and every effort to detach it proved hopelessly ineffectual.

Finally, another boat was let down to the raft in safety. Avery hastened with extended arms eagerly to grasp it. When he reached the edge of the raft, his weight depressed it a little, so that he just missed his grasp of the boat, and fell into the rushing flood, and was borne swiftly downward. On the verge of the cataract, he rises; leaps, in a death struggle, from the flood; throws up his arms; utters a shriek of agony; and is seen no more.

Poor Avery! For eighteen most tedious and most wearisome hours, with alternate hopes and fears, and almost despairing exertions for life, hope, in a moment, fled, and he is at last suddenly swept into the gulf and numbered with the dead.

CHAPTER VIII.

Verge of the Island—Circular Stairway—When and by Whom Constructed—Height from the River—Dismal Descent—Wildness of Scenery—Impending Rocks—Fearful Impressions—Lonely Path—Rills Overhead—Ruins—Little Bird—Foot of the Falls—Awful Impressions—Wrathful Billows—Gulf-Bottom—Scenes at Each Standpoint—Rainbows—Symbols—The Sun's Alchemy—Velocity of the Falling Sheets—Visitors Behind the Falls—Awful Dungeon—Reflections—Man's Noblest Structures—Man Humbled—His Haughtiness Quenched.

BUT to return. The visitor, standing on the verge of Iris Island, between the two Falls, may now step from the edge of the precipice, upon a strong, round tower, or circular stairway (with circular steps inclosed), clamped securely to the rocks, and descend the dizzy flight of steps to the bed of the river on which the mighty torrents fall.

The total descent is one hundred and eighty-five feet. But the staircase is about eighty feet only in height. It was constructed in 1829, by

HORSE SHOE FALL.

Nicholas Biddle, formerly president of the United States Bank.

The mind dreads the dismal descent into this deep river-gorge, where the spectator is hemmed in by precipitous walls of rock, and tumbling ocean-floods. It seems like leaving the living for the dead. The furious river to which he descends, now rejoined, rolls far below, deep and angrily; black with the shadows of scowling hills, craggy banks, and the escarpment of rocks.

Having safely reached the foot of the stairway, into this deep, romantic river-chasm, he now exultingly threads his way along the narrow defiles, beside rocky walls of giddy height, under overhanging cliffs, and the river's edge, to either Fall.

From the Biddle Stairway, we will turn to the left, along the narrow, devious path, strewed with riven rocks, and first reach the foot of the inner, island shore of the Horse-Shoe Falls.

Over his path are bald, impending rocks, refusing a carpet of verdure, seeming to want but the wafting of a zephyr to crush the prisoner, and then be plunged themselves into the unfathomed and unfathomable gulf beneath. These towering cliffs, afar overhead, arouse the dormant powers of the most stupid, as he turns his eye sky-ward, and beholds their awful forms frowning down upon the pigmy that hazards his presence abreast of their terrible powers. Man quails, and pales into insignificance, before incomprehensible powers that ingulf all his thoughts.

Along this lonely path, shrubs and flowers, in highest perfection, lift their bright, luxuriant heads to cheer the desolation, beautify the solitude, and embellish the ruggedness that reigns around. Vines, with brilliant leaves and flowers, creep out of the fissures of the rocks to enjoy the sunshine. Numerous little murmuring rills glide at his feet.

Afar overhead, rippling rivulets trickle through the crevices, or are forced through rents in the rocks, and come scrambling down, in dripping showers, broken into fragments, expended in mist, or blanched into spray-like feathery snow, or filmiest lace, long before they fall upon his path.

Rocks, of many tons weight, fringing the precipices above this foot-path, at immense heights, have thundered down into this rugged glen, choking the defiles between the stairway and each of the Falls. Rocks, thus sundered above, and amassed in confusion in this cragged basin, lie in grand and magnificent ruins. These rocky ornaments slumber here, piled in all conceivable positions, and immensely heighten the combined wildness and grandeur of the scene.

No living thing is seen, save, now and then, a reeling, solitary bird, enshrined in banks of foam, sweeping round in wanton circles; or, on poised wing, it hovers, and tips its pinions in the dreary waste of waters. Darling little bird! how joyously thou lingerest here, amidst the gales that threaten thy destruction.

The spectator still courses his way along over these imposing obstructions to the foot of the Falls. Here he stands, side by side, with the descending floods, and has his first near view of one of the mighty Falls—the Horse-Shoe Falls, between him and the Canada side. He looks up; then casts his eyes forward, and backward, and to either side; but he sees only upward, where the stars shine in the grand temple of the skies, while his senses ache as he sees himself seemingly hedged in, without any mode of egress, where destruction reigns in madness and threatens to ingulf the spectator.

Here, in desolate grandeur, the "Thunder of Waters," through the world's unmeasured cycles, has held undisturbed dominion, gleaming in visions of such terror, magnificence, and beauty, as if to mirror the attributes of Divinity.

Deafening thunders! Awful booming! Down they come, rushing in wildest wrath. What thrills of terror minglé with their awful symphonies!

He gazes afar up, upon the deep, sea-green, terrific masses, which have stormed through untold centuries, as they break over the high verge, or leap from the tremendous ledges. Crash! Loud Thundering! Down they come! They bound furiously, billow pursuing billow, till overwhelmed in smothering ruin, and blanched to purest whiteness. They pour down their wild waves into fathomless chasms, then urge themselves hastily onward to the awaiting ocean. Incessantly raging and storming in angry vehemence, they beat the shore, and fling away, like enraged, irresistible powers, exulting in the magnificence of their own display. Awfully the white-crested billows lash and foam; dash, and are re-dashed in turn; then unite, and sweep on in dread alliance to the peaceful sea. A thundering tumult shakes the basis of the cliffs.

The eye sweeps round for relief from the terror of these presiding powers, but the vision is limited by mountain rocks, awfully grand; ocean-tempests, storm-clouds, angry billows, foaming gulfs, and smoking floods; all scorning down upon the intruder as unfit to stand where omnipotent powers are exerting their energies. Tremblingly he stands on the gulf-bottom, confused and awe-struck, bending down under the overwhelming weight of immensity in which he is intombed.

Gusts of curling spray roll up from the seething waters, till, high in the air, they mingle with the clouds, assume a thousand fantastical shapes, and dissolve in the air. Under the splendors of the sun, the pearly exhalations glitter as if touched with fire. Refulgent, misty globules beautifully intermingle with purple and gold, and flame out like the explosion of golden showers from brilliant fire-works.

Revolving mists lazily smoke round the basement of rocks, or creeping vapors gather in thick folds from the dim margins of the river, then wreathe into a thousand imaginary forms, and depart like one in haste to be gone. Clouds, in wild confusion, wafted by the breeze, or driven by the wind, exult in seas of azure and gold, and gleam with crimson fire.

Each varied standpoint, in keeping with the laws of optics, furnishes new wonders and beauties, and reveals brilliant scenes invisible before. Scores of positions are full of varied, enchanting beauties.

Rainbows, like ethereal spirits hanging over the scene, linger around the spectator, and mantle him in radiant circles as they sweep through the air, tinting the snow-white spray. Gorgeous rainbows! Resplendent in colors! Ye are beautiful, spanning symbols, sublime and divine; vow-symbols at creation from a flood. Ye are symbols, too, of Love, that arches the world's history and prophecy, and unites in divine harmony the Edens of Creation and Redemption.

By the sun's alchemy, the dissolving sheets of foam culminate in combinations of richest tints, which no art can rival. Snowy mists, resplendent with arches of colored light, flash into diamonds, emeralds, sapphires, and pearls, as if to vie with the gorgeous panorama of the skies. The falling sheets strike the floor of the river with a velocity of one hundred feet a second.

Visitors sometimes venture behind the Falls, under the dismal rocks, over which the sheets of Niagara rush with the noise of cannon. Here, shrouded in gloom, desolation and wildness reign alone. When they enter these gloomy caverns, gusts of spray quickly drench their garments through. Hence, dressing-rooms, water-proof dresses, and careful guides, are always at command for those who desire to visit these fearful caverns.

The visitor, now completely arrayed in his water-proof outfit, advances into the dreary dungeon, over the slippery edges of rocks, quivering, and delicately balancing his footsteps between time and eternity. For a moment only he dares gaze upon the furiously surging billows at his feet, raging in whirlpools that mock the tiny opposition of man. Incessant thunders peal out like the explosions of a hundred cannon. What a dilemma for mortals! narrowly imprisoned between impenetrable walls of gloomy rocks and hurling Niagara.

He is hedged in where appalling storm-clouds, wild hurricane-winds and sea-floods, exult on thunder-thrones—fit emblems of eternal power. Down drops the brimful ocean at his feet, crash upon crash, re-echoing, in volleys of thunder from the touching rocks, and stupefying the affrighted spectator who hazards his presence in this Tartarean dungeon, where deep thunders seem to rend the rocks and vaulted skies.

Such displays of power and terror enkindle not only the highest admiration, but fill the mind with awe, inspiring the deepest gratitude to Him by whom such exhibitions of beauty and power are produced. The reflection that, for untold thousands of years, day and night unceasingly, these turmoils of amazing powers have been going on, greatly adds to the interest of the scene. The noblest of human structures fades away into paltry toys before their grandeur, magnificence, and mountain-powers. They transfuse their mightiness into the soul of the beholder.

What a withering sense of insignificance palls the mind under the overwhelming displays of such terrible powers. It quenches his haughtiness, stains and paralyzes his pride. In their presence kings feel uncrowned, and earthly sovereigns humbled, disrobed, and dethroned. Man here is vanquished, and is captive; yielding willing homage to superior, presiding powers.

WHIRLWIND BRIDGE AND ROCK OF AGES—CAVE OF THE WINDS.

CHAPTER IX.

Leaving our Standpoint—Biddle Stairway—Three Falls—Luna Island—Lunar Bow—Origin of the Name—Third, or Central Fall—Foot-Bridge—Cave of the Winds—Origin of the Name—Character of the Rocks—Table Rock—Pressure of Water—Falling Rocks—Dates—Deep Gorge Cut Through Rocks—Dimensions—Falls at Queenstown—Falls Recede—Drain Lake Erie—Dip of the Rocks.

WE now leave our present standpoint, at the bottom of the Horse-Shoe Falls, where we have dwelt so long, and retrace our steps along our lonely little path. On our return to the other (American) Falls, we pass the Biddle Stairway, on which we descended.

It is unnecessary to furnish a separate, protracted outline of the American Falls. The above remarks respecting the Falls, dwelt upon at some length, are equally applicable to both. In a former part of the work, it was stated that the American Falls are about one thousand feet in breadth and one hundred and seventy feet in height.

There are, in fact, three Falls, instead of two. The American Fall is divided by a little island, called Luna Island. It is about one hundred feet from Goat Island, and very near the verge of the cataract. Hence, the third, or central Fall, is about one hundred feet wide.

To my young reader I may say that *luna* is the Latin word for "moon." Luna Island means Moon Island. The island is so named because from it the finest lunar-bow (or rainbow) is seen, in the mist of the Falls, when the moon is full and has a certain altitude.

There is a little foot-bridge that connects Luna and Goat (or Iris) islands. Between these two islands, and at the bottom or floor of the river, is a cavern, called "Cave of the Winds." It is one hundred feet long, thirty feet wide, and one hundred and thirty feet high. The falling sheets of water force the air with great violence into the cavern, and hurl it round like a terrible storm. Hence it is called "Cave of the Winds."

These deep recesses, or caverns, behind the Falls, result from the character of the rocks. The lower rock is a soft shale, which washes out, or rapidly wears away by the confined, storming winds, and the reflex action of the dashing currents. The upper rock is an overhanging, or projecting limestone, called Table Rock, because it is like the leaf of a table. This rock is eighty feet in thickness (upper silurian), and often breaks down under the pressure of ten or twelve millions of tons of water that storm over it every minute.

These vast, projecting plates of rock, thus wrenched from their strongholds, and plunged into the abysmal depths below, are heard and felt with earthquake power.

In 1818, a solid block of rock, one hundred and sixty feet long and forty feet wide, fell, at midnight, with a thundering crash, which was heard at a distance of many miles. The people started from their slumbers, imagining it to be an earthquake.

In 1828, half an acre of rock fell from the centre of the Horse-Shoe Falls.

In 1850, another solid block of Table Rock fell, two hundred feet long, sixty feet wide, and one hundred feet deep. The deafening roar pealed out like the roll of heavy thunder.

Numerous incidents of similar occurrences could be furnished.

The Falls recede at the rate of about a foot a year. The distance between the Falls and Lake Erie is thus continually diminishing. By the unseen erosive action of the Falls, they have scooped or chiseled out, through solid rocks, a gorge, or channel, seven miles long, from twelve hundred to two thousand feet wide, and five hundred feet deep.

This deep gorge is between the Falls and Queenstown. The Falls were doubtless formerly at Queenstown, seven miles below their present location. The opinion prevails that the Falls will recede to the city of Buffalo, and drain the lake. But this cannot be; because the dip of the rocks will soon carry the soft shale so far below the bed of the river that they will cease to be acted upon. Then the hard limestone alone will occupy the whole height of the Falls. Hence, the abrupt Falls will gradually disappear, and a gentle slope will intervene between Lake Erie and Lake Ontario.

THREE SISTERS AND GOAT ISLAND FROM CANADA SIDE

CHAPTER X.

"Sam Patch"—His Leaps—Ladder—Height—His Leap at Genesee Falls, N.Y.—Reflections—Change of Standpoint—Ascend the Tower—Gliding Along the Verge of Goat Island—Moss Islands, or Three Sister Islands—Bridges—Finest View of the Rapids—The Hermit's Cascade—The Stranger's Residence—Subject to Melancholy—Cabin—His Flute—Log Projecting over the Falls—His Delight and Homage—Bathes and Perishes—Leave Sister Islands—Re-Cross Iron Bridge that Spans the Rapids—Declining Day—Return to Niagara Village—Sunset—Domiciled—Beauty of Western Sky—Charming Scenes—Moral Reflections.

JUST at this point, between the Centre Falls and the Biddle Stairway, is where the memorable "Sam Patch" made his two leaps in 1829. He erected a ladder, one hundred feet long, against the rocks, with ropes, the top projecting out over the water. On the bank and the top of the ladder he placed his platform. All things being in readiness, thousands of spectators crowded every point to witness the daring spectacle. "Sam," suitably attired for his "dip," gayly tripped along his narrow platform, at giddy height; tipped his bow to his gazing congregation; and went down, feet first, one hundred feet, into the gulf of waters below.

Not content with his Niagara exploits, he afterwards made a higher leap, of one hundred and twenty-five feet, at Genesee Falls, N. Y. Poor fellow! here he went down, but never rose again. His body has never been found. What vain aspirations for earthly glory! For a little human applause, he risked his life—body and soul. What can it avail him now, since his daring profession has borne him to the regions of the dead. His mind is now engrossed with other scenes than than those he vainly cherished here.

We now leave our present standpoint at the floor of the American Falls, or the foot of Goat Island, and trace our way back along the rugged path to the Biddle Stairway. We ascend its towering height, and are again on Goat (or Iris) Island, well repaid for our toil.

We turn to the right, and thread our way along the verge of the island; pass the Horse-Shoe Falls, keeping the road that fringes the Rapids, to the head of Iris Island. Here are three islands, called Moss Islands, or the Three Sister Islands. They are united to Goat Island by three beautiful bridges.

From these bridges the finest views of the Rapids are seen. The Rapids gallop down under these bridges, hastening to throw themselves over the precipices in white foam into the gulf below.

Between Moss Island and the shore, there is a beautiful little fall, called the Hermit's Cascade.

It was the favorite resort of Mr. Francis Abbot, an entire stranger, who came to the Falls in 1829, and made the island his cherished, permanent residence. Subject to melancholy, he wandered night and day over the island. All his thoughts and feelings were absorbed in Niagara. He never left the Falls. He seemed never to rest.

All his days and nights were spent in gloomy contemplations of the great cataracts. He often bathed in the little cascade; hence its name. He was not talkative, and shunned company. The citizens on mainland, in winter, would see the flickering of his fire on the lonely island, through the seams of the little log cabin he had constructed with his own hands. Sometimes they would hear the sweet tones of his flute mingling with the thunders of the cataracts.

With a fearless, elastic step, he would trip far out over the boiling gulf, fearfully high, on a favorite beam of timber that projected over the Falls. For hours he would pace to and fro on his log, and look down far below from his giddy height, with homage and raptures of delight.

The threatening billows under him, and the grand rhythm of the incessant thunders around him, seemed to chime sublime harmonies with his own feelings.

Some years afterwards he was bathing in the river below the Falls, where his clothes were found. Many days afterwards his body was discovered fourteen miles below, at Fort Niagara; the mouth of the river emptying into Lake Ontario. It was brought back, and buried near the Falls he loved so well.

We now leave the Three Sister Islands, cross Goat Island, pass again over the Iron Bridge that spans the American Rapids, and return to Niagara village (American side), from which we started at the outset.

Our enjoyment was now checked, however, by the reflection that the sun had declined far below the western horizon, and the closing day and twilight were warning us home. The exciting scenes of the day, too, induced feelings of weariness, and suggested the necessity of needful repose. Hence we repaired at once to our hotel, and were comfortably domiciled for the night.

Long after the sun had faded from our vision,

it still beautifully gilded the evening sky, shedding its blush of purple and crimson over the west. Brilliantly colored cloud-bands hung along the horizon, fringing and crowning the distant hill-tops, conferring the richest lustre, and illuminating the whole west. The dark clouds, far above, resting on the sky, more brilliantly set off the refulgent parts. The general, serene loveliness, and soft, delicate hues, were in joined contrast with the scenery of Niagara. These charming scenes remained long in their full glory.

Such grand displays of beauty cannot be witnessed with indifference. They inspire admiration, awaken devout thoughts, call for deepest gratitude, and fill the soul with visions of beauty and Almighty power.

"O Lord, how manifold are Thy works! In wisdom Thou hast made them all: the earth is full of Thy riches."

CHAPTER XI.

Early Dawn—Toilet and Entertainment—Village Street—Beautiful Park—Stately Oaks—Avenues—Promenades—Pleasure-Grounds—Enchanting Views — Concert-Hall—Gateways—Toll—Point-View—Banks and Masonry—Photographing Gallery—Inclined Railway—Length and Breadth—Its Object—Flight of Steps—Safe Descent—Spray Showers—Third Cavern—Ferry-Boat—Battling the Billows—New Suspension Bridge—Its Location and Description—Stairway—Elevator—Tolls.

AS the early dawn unclosed its gates of glory, robing the East in golden beams, we were at our toilet, and early tabled for our morning entertainment, in haste for the various missions of the day.

Leaving the hotel, we descend the street of the village (American side), with a beautiful park on our right. The park is thickly wooded with stately oaks.

The oak is the proud monarch of the wood. There in sublimity he towers in his magnitude and colossal height. He mocks the storm, and frowns upon the tempest. In his robe of royalty, he proudly stands in majestic grandeur, crowning

NIAGARA FALLS FROM POINT PROSPECT—AMERICAN SIDE.

the forest. He is no annual. Scores of decades have looked down upon these regal oaks, donned in their verdant robes, and making, in spring, the grove enchanting with emerald beauty. These luxuriant trees overshadow handsome avenues and beautiful promenades, which in summer form delightful pleasure-grounds.

The park is tastefully laid out in walks and flower-plots. Fashionable drives in carriages, finely attired, make circuits around the park, while every foot-path is a promenade. Wearied visitors, after the exciting scenes and toils of the day, repair in the evening to the beautiful lawns, and refresh themselves in these sylvan retreats.

The park affords a fascinating prospect of the Falls. From its green banks, with all the Falls in full view, the spectator can look down with irrepressible emotions into the deep river-gulf far below. The river rolls on with great violence and power, washing the base of these extended lawns and fragrant bowers, adding not only terror to the scene, but also the romantic charm of perpetual novelty in its surging billows. Banks, fringed with trees, bending over tremendous cliffs and frightful precipices, also add to the grandeur of the scene.

Within the park inclosures a beautiful hall is erected, for concerts, picnic parties, &c. The park contains eight acres, and extends below and above the American Falls.

We now leave Prospect Park; pass through a gateway (fee twenty cents) on our way to Point View. This point of observation is in the immediate vicinity of the American Falls. The position affords a grand, entire view of the three Falls of Niagara.

The scene is beautifully and terribly grand, surpassing all description. The eye sweeps the complete curvature of all the Falls. The ocean-floods; the white, surging billows in angry attitudes of battle array; the deluge dashing away with irresistible power; the towering mountains of spray, and the deafening thunder-tones—all conspire to bewilder the spectator, as he confronts these seemingly unearthly powers.

The bank is here lined with solid masonry and a protecting wall, so that the spectator may safely stand on the verge of the precipice, and gaze down, from his giddy height, upon the turmoil of waters that foam beneath his feet.

Here, also, stands a fine photographing gallery, under the proprietorship of the skilful and accomplished Charles Bierstadt, Esq. Visitors here are finely photographed, the magnificent expanse of the cataracts forming the background in the picture.

Here, also, is the Inclined Railway, whose bed has been cut in the surface of the rocks. A double railway track is laid upon it, on which two cars glide to and fro, ascending and descending at the same time, by a little of the water-power of Niagara. The track is three hundred and forty feet long, and a perpendicular height of one hundred and eighty feet. The design of the railway is to convey passengers from the summit down to the river's edge.

There is also a flight of two hundred and sixty-four steps, along the side of the railway track, for the accommodation of those to descend who are not specially gifted with nerves brave enough to descend a railway sloped at an angle of 32°, over a base of one hundred and sixty feet.

The visitor, having made a safe descent to the foot of the railway, is now at the brink of the river-basin. Here, at the foot of the American Falls, he may ponder and ramble over immense masses of rocks, which have fallen down from the towering heights.

No description can give an idea of the beauty

and grandeur of the Falls from this point. It is perhaps the very finest. He stands almost under the falling floods, while the ocean billows are terribly surging at his feet. The playful zephyrs profusely lavish their showers of spray upon him, crowning him with brilliant mist; and sometimes, when the sun shines, he may reach out his hand, and "catch the rainbow."

Quite recently, at this Point, another cavern has been discovered under the American Falls. It is thought that it can be explored to the distance of one hundred feet.

The visitor here may take a little ferry-boat, and cross the river to the Canada shore. The little boat, like a bubble upon the wave, now plays upon the crests of the billows; then sinks in the deep trough between them. Again, it emerges; climbs the waves; only to be again depressed, and almost hidden from view.

These alternate elevations and depressions of the little boat, very impressively remind the sensitive voyager of the school-boys' play called the "see-saw." Nor does he feel the more comfortable when the oarsman, battling the billows, informs him that he is two hundred and sixty feet from the bottom.

The writer has a very vivid recollection of this

experiment in a little skiff, while an unwearied battle was going on between the stern and bow of the boat for the ascendency. Our little skiff reeled and staggered, as it scaled the billows, struggling on to the distant cliff, which, without any damage, we safely made in triumph.

It is very remarkable to state, that in this mode of ferrying the river here, not a single accident has occurred in sixty years.

There is now, however, a better way of passing over these turbulent waters at this Point. It is by means of the new suspension bridge that spans the river at the ferry.

This bridge is sixty rods below the American Falls, and was built in 1868. It must not be confounded with the lower great railway suspension bridge, which is two miles below the Falls, and will be described hereafter.

The upper, new suspension bridge is for foot passengers and light carriages. It is one hundred and ninety feet above the river, the river itself being two hundred and sixty feet deep. The total height of the bridge, above the bed of the river, is four hundred and fifty feet. It is twelve hundred feet long, spanning the river, and connecting the American and Canada shores.

The bridge is suspended to two iron cables,

nineteen hundred feet long, resting on massive towers. The ends of the cables are securely imbedded in excavations, quarried out of solid rock. The cables are capable of sustaining three thousand tons. The weight of the bridge itself is two hundred and fifty tons. It is a beautiful structure, and one of great admiration.

The three Falls are seen in their grandeur from this bridge. The river comes down in boiling torture, and churned to snowy whiteness. The bridge also furnishes a magnificent view of the stupendous river-rapids, that come down roaring in hoarse thunders, and are ingulfed in their enormous liquid vaults.

Before the construction of the new suspension bridge, passengers from the American side reached the Horse-Shoe Falls (Canada side) principally by way of the lower great suspension bridge—a distance of about five miles. Now, by way of the new suspension bridge, they reach the Falls in a walk of ten or fifteen minutes from the village hotels. Each passenger pays twenty cents toll, whether in carriage or on foot. A one-horse carriage pays thirty-five cents, and a two-horse carriage pays fifty cents toll. It was built by a stock company, under the architectural skill of —— Reefer, Esq., of Ontario.

Stairway and Elevator.

At the terminus of this New Suspension Bridge, on the Canada side, there is a stairway on one side and an elevator on the other. These are grand towers, from which the spectator commands one of the finest views of the Falls, magnificent beyond description.

By means of the stairway and elevator, passengers reach the top of the towers. They enter them on a level with the floor of the bridge. The elevator is Otis's Patent Safety Hotel Elevator.

The car ascends and descends a distance of one hundred feet. It is beautifully panelled and adorned, and set with cut-glass windows. It is rendered very secure by a variety of ingenious, self-adjusting contrivances, so that accidents of any kind are almost impossible.

At the top of the towers is a beautiful room, fifty feet long and twenty feet wide, entirely surrounded by plate-glass windows. Above this room is a promenade deck, surrounded by heavy railing and crowned with a beautiful cupola. The room is entirely inclosed, and amply supplied with chairs for the accommodation of visitors.

The car gently glides to and fro, propelled by steam power.

CHAPTER XII.

The "Maid of the Mist"—Its Terrible and Sublime Mission—In the Spray—Gorgeous Scenes—New Suspension Bridge—Horse-Shoe Falls (Canada Side)—Table Rock—Gulf Basin—Scale of Vastness—Grand Outline—Companion Behind the Falls—Spray—Falling Rocks—Niagara in Winter—Ice Crystals—Configurations—Brilliant Points—Forest of Jewels—Ice Bridge—Feelings of Devotion—Farewell—Apostrophe to Niagara—Legend of the White Canoe—Museum.

The "Maid of the Mist."

A FEW years ago, a gallant little steamer, fitly named the "Maid of the Mist," made short voyages from the lower Railway Suspension Bridge—a distance of two miles—to the Falls. Its design was for the pleasure-trips of passengers, or visitors, who wished to make excursions on the river, and have a near view of the Falls.

It looked like a swan—a thing of life—floating on the bosom of the waters. Laden with precious life, bravely would it career on its native element,

NEW SUSPENSION BRIDGE—NIAGARA

The Falls of Niagara.

proudly exulting in the grandeur of its mission. Now it plunges in a frightful trough; then emerges from its watery grave. Again, it mounts the crests of the surging billows, and gallantly rides over waves, foam, and rainbows. Elated in its sublime yet daring mission, it proudly veered over the billows, up to the very Falls, where the vast sheets pour down their liquid walls, as if they were pinnacled in the sky. It approaches so near the descending floods as to penetrate, and be impearled in, the spray of the Falls.

The scene is most terribly sublime and impressive. The falling rivers, most frightful, come down almost immediately overhead, from the rugged tops of the huge cliffs. Enormous surfs lash the sides of the little steamer, as it is rocked and tossed upon the heaving billows.

Arrayed in terrible wrath, the surging sea groans to be disenthralled from its deep gulf-prison. The roll of heavy thunders reverberating from their imprisoned enclosures, echoes back, only to mingle again with other unceasing turmoils of thunder and foam.

To look down upon the billowy foam bewilders and fills the mind with solemn awe; and to look up, and see the river-floods falling in thunder-tones at his side, greatly deepens the terrible impression. The immense masses of infuriated waters are everywhere surfaced with white foam, like the drifting of snow by the howling storm.

The scene is one of majesty and power, and greatly surpasses all description. It ingulfs all human thought.

Niagara seems to scorn the intrusion of the "Maid"; yet the hovering rainbow greets and beguiles the visitor to its upward, beautiful abode, as it rises, beckons, and is transferred to the bosom of the clouds. Columns of gorgeous spray, majestic cliffs, splendid rainbows, and other sublime exhibitions of surpassing grandeur, shed refulgent glories upon the scene, and outvie the beauty of an Italian sky.

The "Maid of the Mist" not proving a very profitable investment to its owners, they sold it to a Canada firm, with the condition that it should be safely navigated through the Rapids and Whirlpool, and delivered at Lake Ontario.

Captain J. R. Robinson, its pilot, with two aids, undertook this fearful experiment. It was, perhaps, the most hazardous experiment ever undertaken by man. The danger was considered so great that no company would insure their lives for a cent. It created intense excitement for miles around. The river boils in its deep cauldron, and, in abrupt turns, is hurled against rocks, tossing the billows thirty or forty feet high, and rushing onward at the rate of twenty-five or thirty miles an hour.

Strange to say, the daring feat was accomplished in safety, with no other injury to the vessel than the falling of her funnel on the deck, just before entering the Whirlpool.

We now cross the New Suspension Bridge to the Canada side, and file our way along a fine carriage-road up to Table Rock—a distance of about three-quarters of a mile.

Table Rock is a part of the vast shore-rock, and also forms the bed of the river above, or the floor of the Rapids, and overhangs the terrible gulfs. Portions of Table Rock have fallen at various times, so that it is much diminished in size.

This point is the best shore-position for viewing the complete, bold outline of this sublime spectacle. From its platform the visitor commands one grand panorama of the falling sea-floods, towering rocks, threatening precipices, terraced cliffs, islands, and the deep, vast gulf-basin. Down in the gulf-bottom is seen a raging ocean, ever boiling and lashing itself into purest whiteness; rolling billows, angrily flinging away gorgeous fleeces of foam; and rich, boundless profusions of spray, orbed in rainbows of its own grandeur. The emerald sea breaks over the verge, and comes down, as if searching deeper gulfs below. They thunder down over their precipices like mighty avalanches down mountain gorges, or tumbling rivers coming down from the clouds. Now, their thunders swell to the roar of hurricanes, attuned to rhythms of thrilling octaves; then again, we hear the soft mingling of more subdued tones, and choral strains, like harpstrings tuned to angelic harmonies.

Above the Falls, the river has the magnificent expanse of a boiling ocean. Nature has wrought out Niagara on a scale of wonderful vastness, and linked it with surrounding phenomena of imposing and surpassing grandeur. The whole scenery is unrivalled, indescribable, and overwhelming.

It is too replete with magnificence and vastness for the sweep of the eye, or the grasp of the mind. Its expanse is too great for the scope of human vision. Its scenes justly entrance his sensations into adoring admiration and awe.

Fancy finds employment in tracing volumes of tinted mist, that roll up to mountain heights, in a thousand fantastic forms, outvieing the serene grandeur of the western sky. Its entire magnitude bewilders, and is too painfully oppressive for the mind. Involuntarily it recoils from the vision, and seeks relief in ordinary surrounding objects.

If the visitor is naturally endowed with a stern spirit and strong nerves, he may now descend a circular stairway, to the bed of the river; glide along a narrow path that leads behind the Horse-Shoe Falls (Canada side).

I hope my travelling companion will pardon the following incident in his history, should it ever meet his eye, as I withhold his name. He was a gentleman of broadcloth, and inherited his share of State pride. Possessing largely the gift of assurance, he proposes alone to initiate himself behind the sheets of falling water. Without being duly attired for his mission, with an elastic step, he walks boldly and in great state to the dizzy entrance. Without the usual civility of a formal introduction to the presiding powers, he makes his bow only; enters the gloomy cavern, canopied with rocks and sea-floods. He advances a few paces, and is suddenly greeted with furious blasts of wind, clouds of spray, and copious rain-showers that drench him through.

Already thoroughly and unexpectedly soaked, he suddenly halts; philosophizes a little; studies the propriety of a little suffocation; examines his wardrobe, and is surprised at the alchemy of Niagara in so quickly transforming broadcloth into dripping rags; shakes the rills off his beaver; makes an observation or two into the future; looks back to see the extent of his success in exploring Niagara vaults; and concludes that, for the present, a little retreat would be the better part of valor.

He sets his compass for "exit," and is again quickly and safely in sunshine. He returns unroofed, however, as the sporting winds playfully lifted his hat, and laid it under contribution. His voyage was brief, and his surveys quite limited. He said it didn't pay. On his return he seemed greatly chastened and subdued in nerve power; having learned the lesson, in some way, under the rocks and floods, that Niagara has some spray to spare, as well as a small supply of thunder, and also still proposes to be second to none in the manifestations of its powers. The whole experiment of my friend transpired in much less time than I have described it.

Visitors, clad in water-proof dresses, under careful guides, frequently explore these terrible caverns. But, as these explorations have been described elsewhere, a repetition is unnecessary here.

NIAGARA IN WINTER FROM CANADA SIDE

As portions of these overhanging rocks frequently fall, the visits to these caverns are not without danger. A few years ago a portion of Table Rock fell, and only a few minutes before about fifty persons were standing on it.

Niagara in Winter.

Winter often furnishes scenery of great beauty and imposing grandeur. It has charms which do not yield even to those of summer. The deep blue of the sky, the rich purple of the landscape the varied coloring of the distant hills, the russet lawns, the mellow radiance of the moon, the refulgence of the stars, glowing with indescribable beauty, all stir the senses, regale, and inspire us with delight.

What celestial purity there is in the whiteness of snow! What exquisite beauties in the crystal flakes of snow, as they come showering noiselessly and tremulously down through the soft atmosphere! They mantle the whole earth in spotless apparel. When the sun pours down a flood of warm beams and transforms the gleaming flakes, then, if congealed, the world flashes in glittering diamonds.

Niagara in winter, if possible, outvies the summer in beauty and grandeur. The ascending vapor from the Falls coats the trees, rocks, and grounds in purest white. The whole realm is richly wrought in an assemblage of ice-crystals of most beautiful configurations.

Myriads of fantastic ice-figures, and fleeces of frozen mist, attach to the diversified objects in the vicinity of the Falls, presenting a sublime and most enchanting scenery. Trees, infolded in transparent ice and frozen foam, bow gracefully down in their white robes, in willing homage to the presiding powers. Everywhere, as far as the eye can sweep, in its utmost range, it is greeted by objects brilliantly crowned with exquisite ice-crystals.

The islands abound in frozen fogs, or congealed, tinted spray, like glittering star-clusters, or volumes of silvery fleeces, reflecting the plays of the richest prismatic colors.

Nature is enshrined in beautiful robes of ever-varying elegance and splendor. Every branch drips with icicles of crystal beauty. Every twig gleams with sparkling frost-work. Every shrub, bush, and limb, in every conceivable form and magnitude, hangs in richest confusion, and, under the full splendors of the sun, glitters in brilliant colors like prismatic glass-drops from a parlor chandelier. Sparkling hoar-frost is transformed into brilliant diamond points. Rocks in sheeted splendor are incrusted in transparent glass. Every deformed fragment is beautifully incased in richest splendor.

What a forest of jewels! Nothing can be imagined more brilliant and beautiful than the reflections of floods of sunbeams from these radiant scenes.

Immense blocks of ice, in winter, flow down the river from Lake Erie, and gorge the chasm between the Falls and the New Suspension Bridge. This forms an immense ice-bridge, over which hundreds of foot-passengers cross in the months of February and March.

Here nature wields her sceptre with unbounded sublimity and beauty. Unceasing exhibitions of power and grandeur are heard and seen in Niagara's roar of thunder-tones, and purpled imagery. The spectator is subdued in gazing upon the world of waters, the abode of beauty and power, and feels a depth of awe and devotion "in looking up, through nature, to nature's God."

Farewell, Niagara! Still, ever charmed, I must leave thee. Yet thy irresistible fascinations chain me here. I linger, and unwillingly turn, and tear myself away.

Niagara, thou assignest to man a sense of withering insignificance. The lesson thou dost teach, more than humiliates—it annihilates self. Thy greatness bewilders; thy glory charms; thy grandeur exalts.

Imagination in vain lends her wings to chronicle half thy sublimities. Thy majesty wafts the soul upward. The vision of thee, reveals the invisible. To thee, man's noblest structures are but toys. Man's labor soon ceases, and he lies down to rest; but thou rollest on, smiling upon our little life-times, and scorning the scanty period of "three-score and ten," the limit of human expectations. Time writes no wrinkles upon thy brow.

Adieu! Adieu! Niagara. The wayfarer of to-day, who gazes upon thy glory, passes away. But thou remainest the same. Myriads in the afar-off generations shall come, and at thy shrine be enkindled into a deeper and holier worship of Him who formed thee, and who bounds thy angry billows.

Roll on, Niagara! Roll on in splendor through the ages. But know thou, that Time shall disperse thy earth-mists, and thou thyself shalt be hushed into silence when the Divine fiat goes forth, "Time shall be no longer."

Legend of the White Canoe.

In days of old, long before the deep solitudes of the West were disturbed by white men, it was the custom of the Indian warriors of the forest to assemble at the Great Cataract and offer a human sacrifice to the Spirit of the Falls.

The offering consisted of a white canoe, full of ripe fruits and blooming flowers, which was paddled over the terrible cliff by the fairest girl of the tribe who had just arrived at womanhood. It was counted an honor by the tribe to whose lot it fell to make the costly sacrifice; and even the doomed maiden deemed it a high compliment to be selected to guide the White Canoe over the Falls.

But in the stoical heart of the red man there are tender feelings which cannot be subdued, and cords which snap if strained too roughly.

The only daughter of a chief of the Seneca Indians was chosen as a sacrificial offering to the Spirit of Niagara. Her mother had been slain by a hostile tribe. Her father was the bravest among the warriors, and his stern brow seldom relaxed save to his blooming child, who was now the only joy to which he clung on earth.

When the lot fell on his fair child, no symptom of feeling crossed his countenance. In the pride of Indian endurance, he crushed down the feelings that tore his bosom, and no tear trembled on his dark eye, as the preparations for the sacrifice went forward.

At length the day arrived; it faded into night as the savage festivities and rejoicing proceeded; then the moon arose, and silvered the cloud of mist that rose from the turmoil of Niagara.

And now the White Canoe, laden with its precious freight, glided from the bank and swept out into the dread Rapids, from which escape is hopeless. The young girl calmly steered her tiny bark toward the centre of the stream, while frantic yells and shouts arose from the forest.

Suddenly *another* White Canoe shot forth upon the stream, and, under the powerful impulse of the Seneca chief, flew like an arrow to destruction. It overtook the first; the eyes of father and child met in one last gaze of love, and then they plunged together over the thundering cataract into eternity!

The Museum.

The Museum near Table Rock contains a very valuable collection of thousands of specimens from the mineral and animal kingdoms. It has a very fine collection of birds, fishes, &c. The various specimens are very tastefully arranged, presenting a forest scene. The proprietor, Thomas Barnett, Esq., deserves great credit for his tireless exertions in gathering so varied and valuable a collection.

CHAPTER XIII.

Burning Spring—Light and Heat—Chippewa—Battle in 1814—Fort Erie—Battle of Lundy's Lane—General Winfield Scott—His Visit Afterwards— Flowers— Navy Island—Patriots' War—American Sympathy—President's Proclamation—The Steamer Caroline—Seized and Sent Over the Falls—Her Expiring Lights.

Burning Spring.

ABOUT two miles above the Horse-Shoe Falls (Canada side) is the Burning Spring, near the edge of the river. The spring is always boiling. The water is charged with sulphuretted-hydrogen gas. It is always rising to the surface of the water. When a lighted match is applied to it, it takes fire and burns with a pale blue flame, with little light and heat.

Chippewa.

Chippewa is a village two miles and a half above the Falls (Canada side). On the 3d of July, 1814, the American troops, under General

Winfield Scott, crossed the Niagara river, and invaded Canada. They captured Fort Erie, opposite the city of Buffalo, N. Y. Fort Erie having been taken, General Scott, leading the advance, attacked the British at Chippewa (July 5th), and gained a brilliant victory. Both armies, however, suffered much.

Battle of Lundy's Lane.

About one mile and a half from Niagara Falls, at Lundy's Lane, a second battle was fought. This great engagement was fought on the 25th of July, 1814. General Scott commanded the Americans, and General Drummond led the British forces. This was one of the most bloody battles of the war. General Scott had only one thousand men, but he maintained the unequal contest until dark.

A British battery, located on an elevation, was a position the Americans very much coveted. General Scott called Colonel Miller to his side, and asked him if he could take it. "I'll try, sir," was the modest reply. Heading his regiment, he steadily marched up the height and secured the position. Three times the British rallied to recapture it, but were as often repulsed. At midnight they retired from the field. Each side lost about eight hundred men.

This victory, though glorious to the American army, was fruitless of direct results.

Many years afterwards General Scott visited the scene of this engagement in company with some ladies and gentlemen. He feelingly described the fierce battle of that day. He pointed out the tree under which he sat down to rest, when fainting from a bleeding wound—the tree protecting him from the British bullets. He plucked a flower and presented it to one of the ladies, remarking "that it grew in soil once nourished by his blood."

Navy Island.

Immediately below Grand Island, in the Niagara River, is a small island, called Navy Island. It is three or four miles above the Falls, and is memorable for being the rendezvous of some Americans during what was styled the "Patriots' War," in 1837–'38. At that time the rebellion of Canada against England aroused the sympathies of many of the American people. In many places meetings were held, and arms were offered to volunteers.

The President (Martin Van Buren) issued a proclamation, refusing the protection of the United States to any who should aid Canada, and sent General Winfield Scott to the frontier to maintain peace.

The American sympathizers took possession of Navy Island, in the Niagara River, as their headquarters, and hired a steamer, called the Caroline, to carry their provisions and war materials.

The British troops, on the night of December 29, 1837, attempted to seize the Caroline at her anchorage at Schlosser (American side). A desperate battle ensued. But the British succeeded in setting her on fire, and letting her drift over the Falls. Thus closed the military career of the Caroline. She shed more light and glory in her death than in her life. In a flame of fire she went whirling down the terrible Rapids, and took her awful leap over the Falls of Niagara.

The British troops on the Canadian shore, and the "Patriots" on Navy Island, kept up a cannonading for some time. The British force, having been increased, however, dislodged the ardent "Patriots." After some conflicts along the line, they disbanded; thus closing their connection with the "Patriots' War."

CHAPTER XIV.

Blondin the Rope-Walker—Rope over the Gulf-River—Railway Trains—"Dean Swift's Dust"—His Marvellous Feats—Indians—Their Grounds—Their Manufactures—Brilliant Colors—Civilized—The Great Railway Suspension Bridge.

Blondin the Rope-Walker.

IMMEDIATELY below the New Suspension Bridge, sixty rods from the Falls, is the site where the memorable Frenchman, M. Blondin, in 1858, performed his first marvellous feats of rope-walking over Niagara. High in the air, he spanned the deep gulf-river, two hundred and fifty feet above the boiling waters, with a strong rope, giving it the greatest tension possible. He secured the ends to the opposite banks, and prevented its tremulous motion by side-ropes attached to the large main rope and the opposite shores. The rope was about twelve hundred feet long.

The wide circulation of his "bills" gave ample information to the public that, on a specified day,

The Falls of Niagara.   119

they could have the pleasure of witnessing what he was pleased to call his "ascension." The public thus advised, and the memorable day having arrived, the whole region round about, as well as afar off, was astir.

The crowded cars of the long railway trains brought their thousands to gaze upon the wondrous scene. Every visible point along the American and Canada shores was laid under contribution to witness the spectacle.

A mission of benevolence (in a pecuniary way) —"a consideration," for a little of the "dust," as Dean Swift says—was "set on foot." Hats, in plentiful numbers, were "passed round," coveting contributions from the generous public, preparatory to the eventful scenes.

All things now being in readiness, the acrobat sprang from his hiding-place, leaped upon his rope, and in a moment was sailing over the gulf.

To exhibit the skilful exertions of his muscular powers, and display his feats of daring bravery on the grandest scale, he played upon his rope as antically as a spider upon its web. Having no rivals in this kind of entertainment, he made himself perfectly at home on his rope. He balanced himself upon it; fell on it; hung from it by his hands, then by his feet; stood on his head;

dropped himself down to the surging river (itself two hundred and fifty feet deep), then up his rope like a spider; walked over his rope blindfolded in a sack; trundled over a wheelbarrow; and carried a man over on his back.

Many other amusing yet fearful exhibitions of expertness were performed. His fund of rope dexterities seemed to be exhaustless. For several years he made Niagara his headquarters.

The writer visited the Falls a few days after the "ascension," and found the feelings of the community still running at high tide over the scenes of the matchless Blondin.

Indians.

A fragment of a tribe of Tuscarora Indians, some three or four hundred in number, resides in the vicinity of the Falls. They occupy lands, known as the Tuscarora Reservation, containing five or six square miles. They employ themselves somewhat in agricultural pursuits, yet are not forgetful to reserve a little leisure for fishing and hunting.

They make the Falls a place of rendezvous—a general depot, where they vend various articles of their own manufacture. They reap large profits from the crowds of visitors who repair to the Falls. Their skill is displayed in ingeniously carving out pipes and pipe-stems; manufacturing moccasins, shoes, and purses with beads; fans, pin-cushions, needle-cases, canoes, strings and bracelets—all wrought out in brilliant colors. Many of their devices are fanciful, skilfully worked out, grotesquely adorned, and are exposed with fine effect.

Sometimes the walls of the shops have been adorned with paintings representing the characters and events of their mythology. Their shelves are decorated with beautiful patterns, coins in bronze, arms, bows and arrows, and various sculptural designs delineating their festive entertainments—proofs of their ingenuity—Indian artdesigns.

Mingled with their own wares, they have collections of minerals, in richly-colored hues, gathered at the Falls and in the vicinity, rising to the dignity of Indian cabinets.

The Indian delights in grotesque implements and gaudy utensils, painted in a diversity of brilliant colors. A Christian missionary is sustained among them, and it is commendable to state that they are civilized and Christianized.

The Great Railway Suspension Bridge.*

Two miles below the Falls is the lower grand iron Suspension Bridge. It is a model of excellence and power—a noble, magnificent structure of wrought-iron wire, combining great beauty and strength. Suspended in the air, it spans the river-gorge of hideous depth. The bridge is nine hundred feet long and twenty-four feet wide, and capable of sustaining a weight of twelve thousand and four hundred tons. It is two hundred and sixty feet above the river. The depth of the river itself is two hundred and fifty feet; thus making the total height of the bridge above the bed of the river more than five hundred feet.

The bridge is suspended to four enormous ropes formed of iron wires. These iron wires are twisted into huge cables, as thick as a man's body. They are supported by massive towers, composed of ponderous stones, or rocks, firmly clamped together by iron bolts and solid masonry. Two of these towers, one hundred feet high, stand on each bank, and are imbedded in solid rocks.

---

* See Frontispiece.

Scenes Around Them. 123

The bridge hangs under four immense iron cables, by means of other large iron ropes, while the cables themselves rest on the towers. There are two cables on each side, one immediately over the other.

Each huge cable is composed of seven smaller cables, called strands. Each strand is made up of number nine wire. There are five hundred and twenty of these wires in a strand.

Each one of these wires was carried across singly, from tower to tower, by means of an iron pulley, moving to and fro, suspended to an iron cord. The resident citizens speak of the little, buzzing wheel, in its busy mission, playing between the towers, as resembling a spider in the air, spinning its web.

There have been two Suspension Bridges at this point. The first was constructed in 1848, by Mr. Charles Elliot. He offered a reward of five dollars to any one who would get a string across the river.

Boys, having great belief in dollar-power, were active rivals for the prize. Their ingenuity was taxed to the utmost to secure the reward. Kites were "the order of the day." At last, a fortunate youth, aided by a favorable wind, landed his kite on the Canada shore, and received the reward.

This bridge was soon followed by the great Railway Suspension Bridge. It was commenced in 1852, and was completed in 1855, at a cost of five hundred thousand dollars. It was built by the British Government for railway trains, but also sustains, immediately under it, a carriage-road and foot-path. This is suspended twenty-four feet below the train-bridge. It was constructed under the architectural supervision of John A. Robeling, Esq.

The beholder gazes with admiration and wonder upon its skilful architecture, the massive character of the materials, and the grandeur of its design. Its magnitude, beauty of form, and elegance of construction, are all in keeping with the grandeur of the surrounding scenery.

A fine view of the river and Falls is furnished from the Railway Suspension Bridge. At this distance the Falls resemble a great sheet of white satin hanging over the cliffs, or the vision of white flakes in a distant snow-shower. The silvery spray bears up brilliant rainbows, as if to embellish the wardrobe of the skies.

As the train moves cautiously over the bridge, the passenger trembles with fear, as his eye looks down into the dark abyss of waters, as they roll, boil, and foam in savage grandeur far below him.

His mind is oppressed with feelings of deepest emotion. Every bosom is freighted with breathless silence, as the noble engine, in seemingly conscious strength and grandeur, files its long train over the impending danger. In apparent majestic pride the noble bridge splendidly sustains its precious freight, while the magnificent engine safely conveys its valuable burden over the yawning chasm without a quiver.

CHAPTER XV.

Whirlpool Rapids—Whirlpool—Devil's Hole—Bloody Run—Brock's Monument—Queenstown—Lewiston—Indian Village—Youngstown.

Rapids and Whirlpool.

BETWEEN the Falls and Queenstown (Canada side), as before stated, the river has cut a deep gorge, through solid rock, seven miles long, from three hundred to one thousand feet wide, and five hundred feet deep. In this distance the bed of the river has a descent of about one hundred feet, and is urged onward with a velocity of twenty-seven miles an hour.

Queenstown is at the foot of this deep river-gorge, and navigation commences here with Lake Ontario. The narrowness of the river in places, combined with its great velocity, causes the rolling billows to toss up their foam and breakers to the height of thirty or forty feet. The scene is grand, and baffles description.

THE WHIRLPOOL RAPIDS—NIAGARA

The Falls of Niagara.

Two Whirlpool Rapids occur between the Falls and Queenstown. The first begins about two miles from the American Falls, or at the great Railway Suspension Bridge, and continues about a mile.

Sir Charles Lyell, the great English geologist, calculated that fifteen hundred millions of cubic feet of water rushed through this gorge every minute. At the foot of the first Rapids, an angle in the river (Canada side), produces a reflex action in the river, heaping and whirling the waters with terrible impetuosity. This reflex action is called the "Whirlpool." The action of the water here has hollowed a large cavity out of the solid rock.

Below this is another Rapid, of about half a mile in extent.

Devil's Hole.

About three miles below the great Railway Suspension Bridge (American side), is what is called the Devil's Hole. It is a dismal gorge in the bank of the river, between one and two hundred feet deep.

A piece of most terrible Indian strategy occurred here during the French war in 1763. A detachment of British soldiers, more than one hundred in number, were ordered with a large supply of provisions from Fort Niagara to Fort Schlosser. The Seneca Indians at this point laid an ambush for them. When the train arrived here, the numerous savages rushed out of their hiding-places like a whirlwind, and, with terrible yells, poured a volley of bullets into their confused ranks. The soldiers, drivers, horses, and wagons, were hurled over the awful precipice into the yawning gulf below, and were crushed to pieces on the rocks. Two only were left to tell the mournful tragedy.

Bloody Run.

A little brook here falls over the perpendicular precipice. It was red with blood from the above Indian massacre. Hence its name.

Brock's Monument.

On Queenstown Heights, seven miles below the Falls (Canada side), stands Brock's Monument. It commemorates the British General Sir Isaac Brock, who fell here in a bloody conflict, October 13th, 1812. It was erected in 1853. Its height

NIAGARA RIVER LOOKING TOWARD LAKE ONTARIO.

is one hundred and eighty-five feet. On its top stands a statue of the gallant General. From the Monument the scenery of the country, and of Lake Ontario, is magnificent. The river here becomes tranquil, and flows on to Lake Ontario in great beauty and grandeur. It is five miles from the Monument to the Lake.

Queenstown.

Queenstown is a beautiful town situated here, and is memorable on account of the above battle that took place here and in the vicinity.

Lewiston.

Lewiston (American side) is a fine town opposite Queenstown, and is the terminus of the Lewiston, Buffalo, and Niagara Falls Railroad. Three miles from Lewiston is the village of the Tuscarora Indians.

Youngstown.

This is a town (American side) near the mouth of the river, opposite which (Canada side) is Niagara town. The former is guarded by Fort Niagara, and the latter by Fort Massasauga (Canada side).

CHAPTER XVI.

Bascom at Niagara—Description of Niagara by Charles Dickens—Description of Niagara by Professor Tyndall.

Niagara.

- BY REV. HENRY B. BASCOM, D. D.

REACHED Buffalo late in the evening. This is a fine, showy young city. Many things interested me until ten the next morning—the Lake, the harbors, shipping, steamers, the canal with its legion of boats, with all the excitement and bustle of enterprise.

For the first time in my life I set foot on British soil, having crossed at Black Rock into Upper Canada on my way to the Falls. At my right rolled the majestic Niagara, with the waters of Erie, St. Clair, Huron, Michigan, and Superior, on their eternal tour to the ocean. On the left lay a finely cultivated country, until I reached Chippewa.

At five in the evening I reached the pavilion, and was soon at the Table Rock, gazing at the most magnificent spectacle that ever chained the eye of a beholder—a world of water rolling and tumbling in thunder and foam.

As I gazed I felt a depth, a devotion, an unutterable intensity of admiration, that, after two hours, made my brain reel, and so unstrung my nervous system that it was with difficulty I crawled from the verge of the rock, and returned to the pavilion, where, in the portico of the third story, in full view of the Falls, I returned to their contemplation by moonlight, and paced the colonnade in wonder and astonishment, until mere exhaustion drove me, at twelve o'clock, to my room to seek repose.

The next day I continued my exploration of the Falls—crossed the gulf below, and from the American side, and from Goat Island, still gazed on the mighty cataract from fifty different points of view.

The following day I ascended the spiral staircase at Table Rock—a flight of one hundred and five steps; and, provided with a guide, ventured as far under the great falling sheet of water as ever human being had dared to go.

· Divesting myself of my clothing, and belting a

mantle of oil-cloth about me, I penetrated, with difficulty and danger, amid foam and thunder and spray, as far as Termination Rock, one hundred and fifty-three feet under the vast falling column, and then pausing, elevated my eyes to look on the universe of water that was tumbling over me, while a slip of the foot must have precipitated me fifty fathoms into the gulf below, where the angry element was tossing and heaving with infuriate life and uproar.

After a moment's pause I commenced my retreat, and effected my return in safety, thankful to God that my temerity had not been chastened with instant death.

I have seen, surveyed, and communed with the whole!—and awed, bewildered, as if enchanted before the revealment of a mystery, I attempt to write. How shall I essay to paint a scene that so utterly baffles all conception, and renders worse than fruitless every attempt at description?

From Table Rock, the whole indescribable scene, in bold outline, burst on my view. I had heard and read much, and imagined more, of what was before me. I was perfectly familiar with the often-told, the far-traveled story of what I saw; but the overpowering *reality* on which I was gazing, motionless as the rock on which I stood, deprived me of all recollection, annihilated all curiosity, and, with emotions of sublimity till now unfelt, and all unearthly, the involuntary exclamation escaped me, "God of Grandeur! what a scene!"

But the majesty of the sight, and the interest of the moment, how depict them? The huge amplitude of water, tumbling in foam above, and dashing on, arched and pillared as it glides, until it reaches the precipice of the *chute*, and then, in one vast column, bounding, with maddening roar and rush, into the depths beneath, presents a spectacle so unutterably appalling that language falters, words are no longer signs, and I despair giving you any idea of what I saw and felt.

Yet this is not all. The eye and mind necessarily take in other objects as parts of the grand panorama: forest, cliffs, and islands; banks, foam, and spray; wood, rock, and precipice—dimmed with the rising fog and mist, and obscurely gilded with the softening tints of the rainbow. These all belong to the picture; and the effect of the whole is immeasurably heightened by the noise of the cataract, now reminding you of the reverberations of the heavens in a tempest, and then of the eternal roar of ocean when angered by the winds!

The concave bed of the rock, from which the water falls, some two hundred feet, into the almost boundless reservoir beneath, is the section of a circle, which, at first sight, from Table Rock, presents something like the geometrical curve of the rainbow; and the wonders of the grand "crescent," thus advantageously thrown upon the eye in combination, and the appropriate sensations and conceptions heightened by the crash and boom of the waters, render the sight more surpassingly sublime than anything I have ever looked upon or conceived of.

As it regards my thoughts and feelings at the time, I can help you to no conception of their character. Overwhelming astonishment was the only bond between thought and thought; and wild, and vague, and boundless, were the associations of the hour.

Before me, the strength and fullness of the congregated "lakes of the North" were enthroned and concentrated within a circumference embraced by a single glance of the eye! Here I saw, rolling and dashing, at the rate of *twenty-five hundred millions of tons per day*, nearly one-half of all the fresh water upon the surface of the globe!

On the American side, I beheld a vast deluge,

nine hundred feet in breadth, with a fall of one hundred and eighty or ninety feet, met, fifty feet above the level of the gulf, by a huge projection of rock which seems to break the descent and continuity of the flood, only to increase its fierce and overwhelming bound. And turning to the crescent, I saw the mingled rush of foam and tide, dashing with fearful strife and desperate emulation—four hundred yards of the sheet rough and sparry, and the remaining three hundred a deep, sea-like mass of living green, rolling and heaving like a sheet of emerald. Even imagination failed me, and I could think of nothing but ocean let loose from his bed, and seeking a deeper gulf below.

The fury of the water, at the termination of its fall, combined with the columned strength of the cataract and the deafening thunder of the flood, are at once inconceivable and indescribable. No imagination, however creative, can correspond with the grandeur of the reality.

I have already mentioned, and it is important that you keep it in view, the ledge of rock, the verge of the cataract, rising like a wall of equal height, and extending in semicircular form across the whole bed of the river, a distance of more than two thousand feet; and the impetuous flood, conforming to this arrangement, in making its plunge, with mountain weight, into the great horse-shoe basin beneath, exhibits a spectacle of the sublime, in geographical scenery, without, perhaps, a parallel in nature.

As I leaned over Table Rock, and cast my eye downward upon the billowy turbulence of the angry depth, where the waters were tossing and whirling, coiling and springing, with the energy of an earthquake, and a rapidity that almost mocked my vision, I found the scene sufficient to appal a sterner spirit than mine; and I was glad to turn away and relieve my mind by a sight of the surrounding scenery—bays, islands, shores, and forests, everywhere receding in due perspective.

The rainbows of the "crescent" and American side, which are only visible from the western bank of the Niagara, and in the afternoon, seem to diminish somewhat from the awfulness of the scene, and to give it an aspect of rich and mellow grandeur, not unlike the bow of promise, throwing its assuring radiance over the retiring waters of the deluge.—*Life of Bascom.*

Niagara.

BY CHARLES DICKENS.

Between five and six next morning, we arrived at Buffalo, where we breakfasted; and being too near the great Falls to wait patiently anywhere else, we set off by the train the same morning, at nine o'clock, to Niagara.

It was a miserable day; chilly and raw; a damp mist falling; and the trees in that northern region quite bare and wintry. Whenever the train halted, I listened for the roar, and was constantly straining my eyes in the direction where I knew the Falls must be, from seeing the river rolling on towards them, every moment expecting to behold the spray. Within a few minutes of our stopping, I saw two great white clouds rising up slowly and majestically from the depths of the earth. At length we alighted; and then I heard the mighty rush of water, and felt the ground tremble beneath my feet.

The bank is very steep, and was slippery with rain and half-melted ice. I hardly knew how I got down, but I was soon at the bottom, and climbing, with two English officers who were crossing and had joined me, over some broken rocks, deafened by the noise, half-blinded by the spray, and wet to the skin.

We were at the foot of the American Falls. I could see an immense torrent of water tearing headlong down from some great height, but had no idea of shape, or situation, or anything but vague immensity.

We were seated in a little ferry-boat, and were crossing the swollen river immediately before both cataracts. I began to feel what it was; but I was in a manner stunned, and unable to comprehend the vastness of the scene. It was not until I came on Table Rock, and looked—Great Heaven, on what a fall of bright-green water!—that it came upon me in its full might and majesty.

Then, when I felt how near to my Creator I was standing, the first effect, and the enduring one—instant and lasting—of the tremendous spectacle, was Peace. Peace of Mind, tranquillity, calm recollections of the dead, great thoughts of Eternal Rest and Happiness: nothing of gloom or terror. Niagara was at once stamped upon my heart, an Image of Beauty; to remain there, changeless and indelible, until its pulses cease to beat forever.

Oh, how the strife and trouble of daily life receded from my view, and lessened in the distance, during the ten memorable days we passed on that Enchanted Ground! What voices spoke from out the thundering waters! what faces, faded from the earth, looked out upon me from its gleaming depths! what heavenly promise glistened in those angels' tears, the drops of many hues, that showered around, and twined themselves about the gorgeous arches which the changing rainbows made!

I never stirred in all that time from the Canadian side, whither I had gone at first. I never crossed the river again; for I knew there were people on the other shore, and in such a place it is natural to shun company.

To wander to and fro all day, and see the cataracts from all points of view; to stand upon the edge of the Great Horse-Shoe Fall, marking the hurried water gathering strength as it approached the verge, yet seeming, too, to pause before it shot into the gulf below; to gaze from the river's level up at the torrent as it came streaming down; to climb the neighboring heights and watch it through the trees, and see the wreathing water in the rapids hurrying on to take its fearful plunge; to linger in the shadow of the solemn rocks, three miles below, watching the river as, stirred by no visible cause, it heaved and eddied and awoke the echoes, being troubled yet, far down beneath the surface, by its giant leap; to have Niagara before me, lighted by the sun and by the moon, red in the day's decline and gray as evening slowly fell upon it; to look upon it every day, and wake up in the night and hear its ceaseless voice: this was enough.

I think in every quiet season now, still do those waters roll and leap, and roar and tumble all day long; still are the rainbows spanning them a hundred feet below. Still, when the sun is on them, do they shine and glow like molten gold. Still, when the day is gloomy, do they fall like snow, or seem to crumble away like the front of a great chalk cliff, or roll down the rock like dense white smoke. But always does the mighty stream appear to die as it comes down, and always from its unfathomable grave arises that tremendous ghost of spray and mist, which is never laid—which has haunted this place with the same dread solemnity since Darkness brooded on the deep, and that first flood, before the Deluge—Light—came rushing on Creation at the word of God.—*Carleton's New Illustrated Edition.*

Prof. Tyndall at Niagara.

On the first evening of my visit, I met, at the head of Biddle's Stair, the guide to the Cave of the Winds. He was in the prime of manhood—large, well built, firm and pleasant in mouth and eye. My interest in the scene stirred up his, and made him communicative. Turning to a photograph, he described, by reference to it, a feat which he had accomplished some time previously, and which had brought him almost under the green water of the Horse-Shoe Fall. "Can you lead me there to-morrow?" I asked. He eyed me inquiringly, weighing, perhaps, the chances of a man of light build and with gray in his whiskers in such an undertaking. "I wish," I added, "to see as much of the Fall as can be seen, and where you lead I will endeavor to follow." His scrutiny relaxed into a smile, and he said, "Very well; I shall be ready for you to-morrow."

On the morrow, accordingly, I came. In the hut at the end of Biddle's Stair I stripped wholly, and redressed according to instructions—drawing on two pairs of woolen pantaloons, three woolen jackets, two pairs of socks, and a pair of felt shoes. Even if wet, my guide urged that the clothes would keep me from being chilled, and he was right. A suit and hood of yellow oil-cloth covered all. Most laudable precautions were taken by the young assistant of the guide to keep the water out, but his devices broke down immediately when severely tested.

We descended the stair; the handle of a pitchfork doing in my case the duty of an alpenstock. At the bottom, my guide inquired whether we should go first to the Cave of the Winds, or to the Horse-Shoe, remarking that the latter would try us most. I decided to get the roughest done first, and he turned to the left over the stones. They were sharp and trying. The base of the first portion of the cataract is covered with huge boulders, obviously the ruins of the limestone ledge above. The water does not distribute itself uniformly among these, but seeks for itself channels through which it pours torrentially. We passed some of these with wetted feet, but without difficulty. At length we came to the side of a more formidable current. My guide walked along its edge until he reached its least turbulent portion. Halting, he said: "This is our greatest difficulty; if we can cross here, we shall get far toward the Horse-Shoe."

He waded in. It evidently required all his strength to steady him. The water rose above his loins, and it foamed still higher. He had to search for footing amid unseen boulders, against which the torrent rose violently. He struggled and swayed, but he struggled successfully, and finally reached the shallower water at the other side. Stretching out his arm, he said to me, "Now come on." I looked down the torrent as it rushed to the river below, which was seething with the tumult of the cataract. De Saussure recommended the inspection of Alpine dangers with the view of making them familiar to the eye before they are encountered; and it is a wholesome custom, in places of difficulty, to put the possibility of an accident clearly before the mind, and to decide beforehand what ought to be done should the accident occur. Thus wound up in the present instance, I entered the water. Even where it was not more than knee-deep, its power was manifest. As it rose around me, I sought to split the torrent by presenting a side to it; but the insecurity of the footing enabled it to grasp the loins, twist me fairly round, and bring its impetus to bear upon my back. Farther struggle was impossible; and, feeling my balance hopelessly gone, I turned, flung myself toward the bank I had just quitted, and was instantly swept into shallower water.

The oil-cloth covering was a great incumbrance; it had been made for a much stouter man, and, standing upright after my submersion, my legs occupied the centres of two bags of water. My guide exhorted me to try again. Prudence was at my elbow, whispering dissuasion; but, taking everything into account, it appeared more immoral to retreat than to proceed. Instructed by the first misadventure, I once more entered the stream. Had the alpenstock been of iron it might have helped me; but, as it was, the tendency of the water to sweep it out of my hands rendered it worse than useless. I, however, clung to it by habit. Again the torrent rose, and again I wavered; but, by keeping the left hip well against it, I remained upright, and at length grasped the hand of my leader at the other side. He laughed pleasantly. The first victory was gained, and he enjoyed it. "No traveler," he said, "was ever here before." Soon afterward, by trusting to a piece of drift-wood which seemed firm, I was again taken off my feet, but was immediately caught by a protruding rock.

We clambered over the boulders toward the thickest spray, which soon became so weighty as to cause us to stagger under its shock. For the most part nothing could be seen; we were in the midst of bewildering tumult, lashed by the water, which sounded at times like the cracking of innumerable whips. Underneath this was the deep, resonant roar of the cataract. I tried to shield my eyes with my hands, and look upward; but the defence was useless. My guide continued to move on, but at a certain place he halted, and desired me to take shelter in his lee and observe the cataract. The spray did not come so much from the upper ledge as from the rebound of the shattered water when it struck the bottom. Hence the eyes could be protected from the blinding shock of the spray, while the line of vision to the upper ledges remained to some extent clear. On looking up over the guide's shoulder I could see the water bending over the ledge, while the Terrapin Tower loomed fitfully through the intermittent spray-gusts. We were right under the tower. A little farther on, the cataract, after its first plunge, hit a protuberance some way down, and flew from it in a prodigious burst of spray; through this we staggered. We rounded the promontory on which the Terrapin Tower stands, and pushed, amid the wildest commotion, along the arm of the Horse-Shoe, until the boulders failed us, and the cataract fell into the profound gorge of the Niagara River.

Here my guide sheltered me again, and desired me to look up. I did so, and could see, as before, the green gleam of the mighty curve sweeping over the upper ledge, and the fitful plunge of the water as the spray between us and it alternately gathered and disappeared. An eminent friend of mine often speaks to me of the mistake of those physicians who regard man's ailments as purely chemical, to be met by chemical remedies only. He contends for the psychological element of cure. By agreeable emotions, he says, nervous currents are liberated which stimulate the blood, brain, and viscera. The influence rained from ladies' eyes enables my friend to thrive on dishes which would kill him if eaten alone. A sanative effect of the same order I experienced amid the spray and thunder of Niagara. Quickened by the emotions there aroused, the blood sped exultingly through the arteries, abolishing introspection, clearing the heart of all bitterness, and enabling one to think with tolerance, if not with tenderness, on the most relentless and unreasonable foe. Apart from its scientific value, and purely as a moral agent, the play, I submit, is worth the candle. My companion knew no more of me than that I enjoyed the wildness; but, as I bent in the shelter of his large frame, he said:

Scenes Around Them.

"I should like to see you attempting to describe all this." He rightly thought it indescribable. The name of this gallant fellow was Thomas Conroy.

We returned, clambering at intervals up and down so as to catch glimpses of the most impressive portions of the cataract. We passed under ledges formed by tabular masses of limestone, and through some curious openings formed by the falling together of the summits of the rocks. At length we found ourselves beside our enemy of the morning. My guide halted for a minute or two, scanning the torrent thoughtfully. I said that, as a guide, he ought to have a rope in such a place; but he retorted that, as no traveler had ever thought of coming there, he did not see the necessity of keeping a rope. He waded in. The struggle to keep himself erect was evident enough; he swayed, but recovered himself again and again. At length he slipped, gave way, did as I had done, threw himself flat in the water toward the bank, and was swept into the shallows. Standing in the stream near its edge, he stretched his arm toward me. I retained the pitchfork handle, for it had been useful among the boulders. By wading some way in, the staff could be made to reach him, and I proposed his seizing it. "If you are sure," he replied, "that, in case of giving way, you can maintain your grasp, then I will certainly hold you." I waded in, and stretched the staff to my companion. It was firmly grasped by both of us. Thus helped, though its onset was strong, I moved safely across the torrent. All danger ended here.

We afterward roamed sociably among the torrents and boulders below the Cave of the Winds. The rocks were covered with organic slime which could not have been walked over with bare feet, but the felt shoes effectually prevented slipping. We reached the Cave and entered it, first by a wooden way carried over the boulders, and then along a narrow ledge to the point eaten deepest into the shale. When the wind is from the south, the falling water, I am told, can be seen tranquilly from this spot; but, when we were there, a blinding hurricane of spray was whirled against us. On the evening of the same day, I went behind the water on the Canada side, which, I confess, struck me, after the experience of the morning, as an imposture.—*Popular Science Monthly.*

www.ingramcontent.com/pod-product-compliance
Lightning Source LLC
Chambersburg PA
CBHW030346170426
43202CB00010B/1267